W9-ACF-711

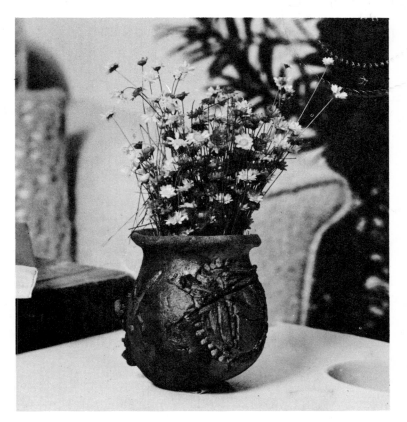

STEP-BY-STEP
ceramics

A Complete Introduction to the Craft of Ceramics

By Jolyon Hofsted

Conceived and edited by

William and Shirley Sayles

 GOLDEN PRESS · NEW YORK

WESTERN PUBLISHING COMPANY, INC.
Racine, Wisconsin

FOREWORD

The craft of ceramics, growing as it has on both avocational and professional levels since the end of World War II, has developed a myriad of new facets. One of these is the reflection in many potters' efforts of the current expressions in painting and sculpture. This is true of the work of Jolyon Hofsted, the author of this book and one of the United States' outstanding young craftsmen. The pots which come from his studio have broken the molds of convention to become fresh, spontaneous expressions of the exciting age in which we live. This same spirit, also contained in the content of this book, imbues his classes in ceramics at The Brooklyn Museum Art School, Queens College, and such summer institutions as Haystack Mountain School of Crafts. The beginner in the field of pottery could not be in better hands. The chapters that follow give you not only the fundamentals of ceramic techniques, practical advice on tools and equipment, and a prodigious number of full-color illustrations, but a series of imaginative projects which can be done at home with a minimum of equipment—and which allow room for and encourage individual experimentation. The craft of pottery is one of the most challenging of all the hand arts, and under the guidance of Jolyon Hofsted you are off to a most auspicious start.

Hal Halverstadt

Managing Editor, CRAFT HORIZONS

Library of Congress Catalog Card Number: 67-13488

contents

INTRODUCTION 4

BASIC PRINCIPLES

The Slab 12
The Coil 12
Slab and Coil 13
Wheel Throwing 13
The Press Mold 14
Slip Casting 14
Sand Casting 15
Egyptian Paste 15
Texture 16
Clays 18
The Firing Process 20
Glaze 22

THE WORKSHOP 24

PREPARATION OF CLAY 26

TEXTURE 28

MAKING PLASTER STAMPS 30

PORTFOLIO PROJECTS

Pinch Pot 32
Slab Portfolio 35
    Weed Holders 36
    Trivets 37
    Cylindrical Vase 38
    Ideas for the Slab Method 40
    Covered Jar 42
    Garden Lantern 46

Coil Portfolio 48
    Cream Pitcher 50
    Patio Bottle 52
    Hanging Lamp 54
Press Mold Bowl and Hot Plate 56
Slip Cast Dinner Plates 58
Press Mold Mugs 60
Sand Cast Weed Pot 62
Combined Methods Portfolio 64
    Candle Holder 66
    Small Vase 68
    Teapot 70-73
Egyptian Paste Jewelry 74
THE POTTER'S WHEEL 76
WHEEL PORTFOLIO 78
    Wheel Throwing 80
    Removing the Pot 82
    Variations 82
GLAZING 84
FIRING A KILN 86
BUILDING YOUR OWN KILN 87
DECORATING TECHNIQUES 88
RAKU 90
    TECHNICAL NOTES 92
    GLOSSARY 93
    SCHOOLS 94
    BIBLIOGRAPHY 95
    SUPPLIERS 95

acknowledgments

In the course of preparing this book many craftsmen were asked for photographic examples of their work, and their cooperation was very gratifying—thanks go to them and to the Brooklyn Museum of Art and to the American Craftsmen's Council for lending photographic material from their collections.

Special thanks are also due to those who have assisted in the preparation of this book:

Hal Halverstadt, *Consultant*
Betty MacDonald, *Design*
Louis Mervar and James Dura, *Photography*
Robert Beame, *Artist*
Olivia Buehl, *Picture Research*

introduction

The most popular of all handcrafts in the U.S.A., on both professional and avocational levels, pottery has seen a phenomenal growth since the end of the Second World War. Statistically, this is reflected by the ever increasing numbers of ceramics courses offered by colleges and universities, museum schools, and art and crafts centers; and by the predominance of ceramics in the hundreds of craft exhibitions held throughout the country each year. Artistically, it is seen in the high level of traditional ware produced by American potters as well as the more avant-garde expressions which parallel the current developments in painting and sculpture. The reasons for this are many, but probably the foremost is the sheer excitement of the process—the transmutation of earth and water by fire to a hard, strong substance with qualities of remarkable endurance.

The growing interest in handcrafts—not just pottery but all the hand arts—is the result of our need for the individual element, the human touch, in this age of mass production and standardization. Although the composition may be finer, the same clay used by potters to make unique bowls, vases, wall panels, and ceramic sculptures is used to construct the look-alike skyscrapers on the rise in America's major cities as well as the drainage tile, plumbing fixtures, and electric insulators that make up the vascular systems of these structures. But this is part of the fascination of clay: that this inexpensive material, dug from the earth and refined, then mixed with water, can with a complex of equipment be molded into the shapes of industrial America and with an absolute minimum of tools be made into objects of aesthetic distinction that often take their places with the art achievements of history.

Right: Greek Attic black figure amphora, about 530 B.C. Incised decoration with touches of red and white paint. The Eugene Schaefer Collection. Courtesy of the Newark Museum.

Early Egyptian vase illustrates the enduring character of pottery. Detail of wall painting depicting vase being made. Tomb of Rekhmara, about 1475 B.C. Courtesy of the Brooklyn Museum and the Bettmann Archive.

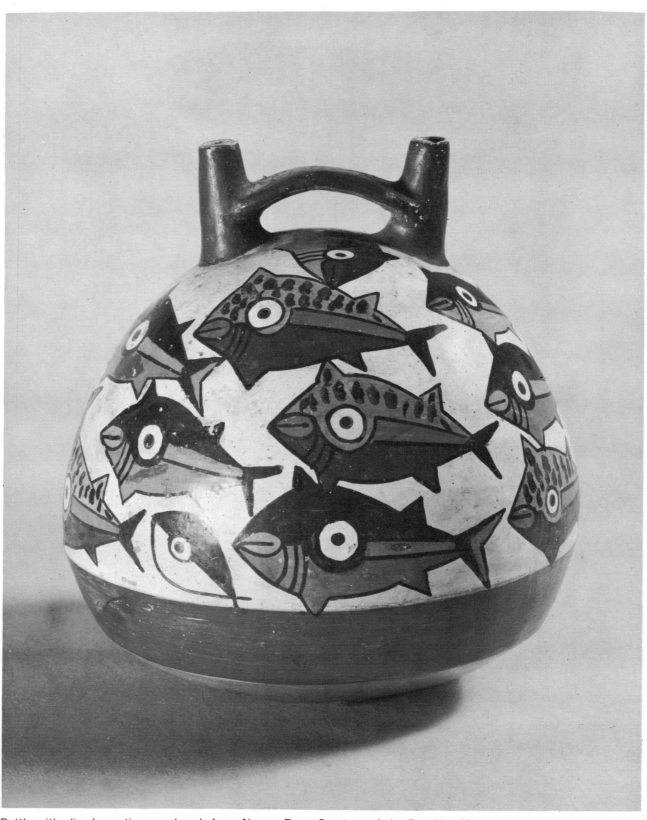

Bottle with slip decoration, unglazed, from Nazca, Peru. Courtesy of the Brooklyn Museum.

Chinese Neolithic vase with slip decoration, un-glazed. Courtesy of the Brooklyn Museum.

American Indian jug, with slip decoration, un-glazed, from Chaco, New Mexico 900–1400 A.D.

Clay is one of the oldest of all craft mediums and dates back to prehistoric cultures. Originally forms were built up free-hand or on a simple mold and dried in the sun. A variety of outer coatings were added to minimize porosity. With the discovery of fire, it was found that by placing clay vessels on a bed of coals they became much less fragile and, in turn, able to withstand heat. The potter's wheel to form objects and the kiln for firing were subsequent technical improvements, and, with the exception of the refinement of these and the research in glaze development, the methods of pottery making have not changed over six thousand years.

Style, on the other hand, has been the variable factor. The early ware made by the potters of East and West were vessels of coarse, impure, roughly textured clay sometimes with painted decoration. As glaze was invented, the decorative possibilities of ceramics expanded. The medium reached a pinnacle in the ancient world with the vases produced in Athens and the surrounding region, called Attica. These ceramic masterpieces were the product of inspired collaboration between potter and painter; the latter creating in glaze the dynamic figure drawings which have remained a powerful influence on Western art from before the Age of Pericles to Picasso. At the opposite end of the spectrum in the history of European ceramics were the elaborately modeled porcelain figures of the eighteenth century. These were created by both European and Oriental potters for display in European palaces. Although Eastern potters continued to produce work of distinction, ceramics became as overblown as the societies that produced it.

Polychrome Delft plate, Dutch c. 1700. Typical of the period when decoration dominated form. Courtesy of the Brooklyn Museum.

With the industrial revolution, pottery went on the production line. The ware turned out in the 1860's was profusely decorated with decal imprinted scenes of sailing ships and flora and fauna, all with limited or no aesthetic value. Artists were the first to react to this treatment of a once noble craft and began dabbling in the medium themselves, first in designing and decorating, but then in actual potting. By the time arts and crafts societies were organized in the 1880's, pottery was a popular craft for artists, who quite naturally looked to the Orient. After the First World War, however, interested craftsmen attending the pioneering Bauhaus school of design opened in Berlin sought out a local folk potter who taught them ceramics in a revolutionary way. He and his students began producing traditional, functional wares in simple techniques that were not unlike the earliest recorded pottery, and, in their reassessment of the direction ceramics was taking, were in great part responsible for restoring the medium to one of distinction.

In the U.S. today, the aesthetic of primitive and folk pottery is the closest of all types of contemporary taste. Using techniques that reflect their knowledge and understanding of the history of pottery, modern ceramists have tended to use clay bodies which offer the most interesting textures, often finding these decoration in themselves, without the need of glaze or other treatments. With the exception of a stream of the avant-garde ceramists who have revived the use of metallic lustre glazes and other materials to create eye-stopping Pop art in clay, the trend is away from decoration for decoration's sake to an exploration and revelation of the basic qualities of clay and glaze.

Another direction in modern American ceramics is toward the unique, one-of-a-kind object. Although there are still many outstanding potters who are involved in production ware, it is becoming

Typical salt-glazed stoneware crock, by Edmands & Co., Massachusetts, c. 1850–1868.

Earthenware Victorian pitcher with all-over relief pattern. By E. & W. Bennett, Baltimore, 1832. Courtesy the Brooklyn Museum.

more and more apparent that handmade pottery for utilitarian use is an anachronism. Mass production and the new materials of industry have been able to give the American consumer a range of handsome functional ware at such economical prices that the U.S. potter today cannot afford to compete in this area. Although possibly against his will, he has been freed from producing repetitive pieces and can today take his craft in any one of a thousand directions. And the range of work he is producing is truly great: from handsome, sturdy one-of-a-kind casseroles and storage jars, to monumental murals in clay, to the most abstract sculptural forms.

As a beginner, with this book you will do a variety of projects ranging in size from a small trivet to a large garden bottle; you will learn the basic terminology of the medium, the hand-building techniques, and the wheel method. This experience with ceramics will not turn you into a professional potter, but it will teach you to know clay and open up some of its possibilities and the directions you may want to take. Clay affords the amateur and professional alike a way of expressing themselves with their hands—and with an inexpensive material.

Earthenware "Art Nouveau" vase in "cucumber green," 8" high. Made by the Grueby Faience Co., Boston, 1897. Courtesy the Brooklyn Museum.

Contemporary wheel-thrown bottles and plate with simple brush decoration by Toshiko Takaezu. Photo by Barney Burstein.

Hand-built slab and coil teapots of unusual design, by James Leedy, illustrate the contrast between the work of today's craftsmen and that of mass-produced wares.

Slab built pot by Beverly Aldrich.

Large coil bottle, unfired, by the author.

the slab

A slab of clay is exactly what the term implies, a ball or hunk of clay rolled out to an even thickness with a large dowel or rolling pin, and the rough edges trimmed off. Much of the contemporary pottery that you see in shops and exhibitions is, in fact, made from slabs joined together, and this forming technique, along with coil-building, is the basis of the projects in this book. In working with the slab (pages 34–47), you will find that it lends itself not only to geometric shapes but also to more spontaneous ones, such as the vase above. This pot was made of six slabs—two for the bottom half, two for the upper section, and two for the handles.

the coil

The technique of coiling goes back in time as far as pottery itself and is the process which eventually led to the wheel method. With the hands, clay is rolled into long coils which are joined and circled round and round to build a vessel or other form. In the top photograph, I have worked the coils one quarter of the way up of what will be a large coil jar about three feet high. This pot was formed in little less than an hour. The beginning potter could work just as quickly, but with this exception the coil projects in this book (pages 49–55) are more modest in scale, since the work you make will have to be fired in the kiln size available to you.

Small vase by R. L. Rosenbaum.

Wheel-thrown casserole by Karen Karnes.

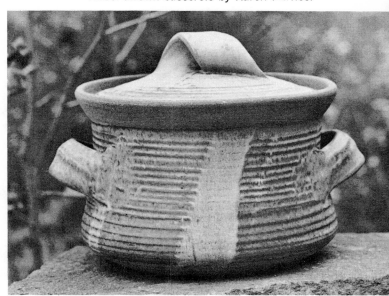

combining slab and coil

Since the two major approaches to hand-built pottery are slab and coil, I would like to point out how well these methods can be combined. A good example is the pot above made from the slabs and coils in the photograph at the top of the page. (In the upper photograph left hand corner is a hand-carved plaster stamp, used to decorate the pot.) The body is slab-built, and the decoration pieces of coil and stamping. Later when you learn how to throw on the wheel, you can add a wheel-thrown spout to a slab bottle, slab handles to a thrown vase, etc. The variations are limitless (Combined Methods projects pages 65–73).

wheel throwing

To watch an experienced potter throw a ball of clay onto the spinning potter's wheel and then to see him manipulate and control the plastic material so that it literally grows into a full-blown form is an exciting and sometimes awe-inspiring experience. As you become more involved with the craft of pottery you will eventually want to learn wheel throwing yourself. One of the advantages of this method is that forms can be shaped rapidly and, with practice, they can be easily duplicated. The step-by-step demonstration on pages 80–82 will help to acquaint you with the basic procedures of this exacting process.

Press mold trivet by the author.

Plate made in the slip cast method.

the press mold

There are several ways of making pottery in molds in order to repeat shapes, such as bowls or mugs, or flat shapes with rich surface decoration such as tiles of the hot plate shown above. One of the most direct is the press mold method in which a slab of clay is laid over a plaster mold and pressed onto it (pages 56–57). The excess clay is then trimmed away, the surface smoothed, and the clay form removed. The mold to make the hot plate, shown above, was made from a slab of hardened plaster with the shape carved out. A molded form though repeated many times can still retain a fresh and individual look by applying additions such as handles or pedestals, textures or glazes.

slip casting

In factory production, slip casting molds are used to make objects such as dinner plates in exact duplicate—with the decoration also standardized. However, this process is also used by the hand potter as a short cut to sturdy plates or platters which can then be finished individually (pages 58–59), usually with painted glazes. A slip casting mold, which can be purchased, consists of two halves, made of plaster, with a cavity in between. Slip, which is liquid clay, is poured into the space inside. After the slip has hardened, the plate is removed from the mold. Slips are available from any ceramic supply house and come in a wide range of colors.

Weed pot made in the sand cast method.

Necklace by Frances Schneider.

sand casting

Sand casting, another popular mold technique (see pages 62–63), allows you to make large, strongly textured pieces, such as the garden bottle above, and to repeat what you have made. For this or other container shapes, a model for *half* of the form is built up in wet sand and the surface textured with a blunt stick or other tool. Layers of plaster are poured over the sand mold and allowed to harden. A slab of clay is laid over the inside of the shell and pressed into it. After the clay has stiffened enough to hold its shape, it is removed, and the process repeated. To make the weed pot, the two halves that are made are joined by scoring them, adding slip and pressing them together.

Egyptian paste

Egyptian paste is a kind of clay that duplicates closely the material from which the ancients made their ceramic beads. Jewelry can also be made with regular clay, but this must be dried, then bisque-fired, glazed, strung on nichrome wire, and fired again. Egyptian paste needs only to be shaped and fired. There are two formulas on page 74, one giving you a dry, matte surface, the other a glossy surface. The materials can be purchased from any ceramic supplier. Egyptian paste can be handled in the same fashion as regular clay: it can be rolled, made into slabs, patted, pinched, or any of the other various forming methods from which beads can be cut or otherwise made.

(Top left) Texture achieved by uniform pinching. Stoneware covered jar, 9″ high, by Marlis Schratter.

(Top right) All-over carved design supplies textural interest. Vase by C. H. Brown. Photo by Judith Gefter.

(Right) Unglazed rough-textured clay produces its own texture. By Robert Winokur.

(Bottom) Example of slab construction lending textural excitement. Bottle by Louis B. Raynor. Courtesy of the Smithsonian Institute.

texture

When the basic form of a pot has been made either with slabs, coils, on the wheel, in a mold, by casting, or with a combination of these, there are two ways of decorating or finishing it. The surface of the clay can be textured, or the entire pot, or parts of it, can be glazed. Texturing is a blanket term for the processes that give variation to the clay surface; some of the methods used are carving, scratching, stamping, adding coils, slabs, or bits of clay. Tools can be any that do the proper job, from a professional sgraffito tool to pencils, nails, or your hands. Even such basic means as pinching can be effective on certain forms. As you can see in the illustrations here, texture can enhance a shape, or it can dominate it.

(Top right) Rough-textured stoneware with white slip and a carved motif. By Sophia and John Fenton. Photo by Brigadier Studios.

(Bottom left) Hand-built vase with rough-textured clay and brushed decoration. By Sophia and John Fenton.

(Bottom center) An example of decoration built up with additional clay. Vase by Gertrud Englander.

(Bottom right) Partially glazed bottle with stamp incised decoration. By Robert Winokur.

clays

Clay, the basic raw material of pottery, is plentiful and inexpensive. There are clay beds in many parts of the country where clay is mined not so much for pottery as for industrial uses. In fact, over fifty million tons of clay were mined for these purposes in 1966. Most clay, as it comes from the ground, is full of impurities and is mixed with rocks, pebbles, and sand. It must, therefore, be refined before it can be used by industry or the potter. Many craftsmen enjoy digging their own clay and processing it, but since this is such a time-consuming operation, and good, reasonably-priced clay bodies are available almost everywhere, we will concentrate on their use rather than on how to prepare them.

What is clay? Essentially, it is granite-type rock that has decomposed into tiny particles over millions of years. It is found in the same position as the parent rock—these are known as residual clays— or in the bottoms of lakes and lagoons, the particles having been washed there from the high rock formations—these are known as sedimentary clays. The plasticity or workability of clay is of primary importance to the potter, and the fineness of the individual clay particle has much to do with its

(Left) Stoneware teapot, wheel-thrown and partially glazed. By Karen Karnes. Photo by Henry Ries.

(Right) Earthenware vases, the one in rear with sgraffito decorations, by Nancy Boyd. Photo by Hans van Nes.

plasticity. Since the original particle size of the sedimentary clays was small enough to have been carried by water, these are finer, and therefore more plastic, than the residual type. It is the sedimentary ones which make up the bodies that you will use.

Before we list the various sedimentary clays, let us take a look at one of the most important steps in the craft of pottery—the firing process. After you have finished making a pot, the next step is to let it dry completely, so that all moisture is gone from the clay. The pot is then placed in a kiln or furnace which is heated to temperatures ranging from 1200° to 2300° F., depending on the type of clay body from which the pot was made. This is called firing,

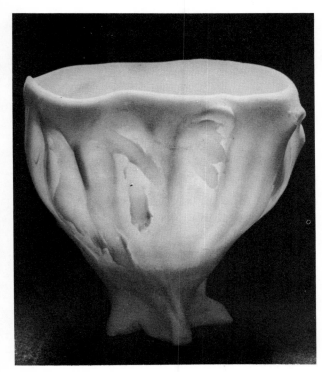

High-fired porcelain bowl, unglazed, 10″ high, by Rudolf Staffel. Courtesy of Craft Horizons.

and the object here is to heat the elements which comprise the clay to the point where they fuse. The color of clay is also transformed during this process and what you had known in the workshop as a dull gray becomes a warm and appealing off-white buff, tan or dark red. Fired clay always has a matte surface; the glossy surface that you have seen on pottery is called glaze, and this will be discussed shortly.

Primary among the sedimentary clays are the following: kaolins, ball clays, fireclays, stoneware clays, and earthenware clays. Most generally used by U.S. potters today are stoneware clays which generally fire to a light gray color and mature between 2280° and 2300° F. These result in ware that is hard and vitreous, ideal for pots that must be handled a great deal or withstand heat, such as cooking ware. Also in general use but not fitting into the above categories are slip clays, usually of glacial origin and found in a limited number of places, primarily Michigan and New York. This is a natural clay which functions as glaze and is also used to help cement joins in slab construction.

Kaolin sedimentary kaolin is a natural clay composed mainly of silica and alumina and when formed makes the finest whiteware body available. It withstands a very high degree of heat.

Ball clay resembles kaolin in chemical content, but is finer and more plastic. When fired, it almost is white.

Fireclay resembles kaolin in chemical content, but contains more iron causing the clay to turn buff-colored when fired. Its endurance of high heat enables it to be used as firebrick and as lining and shelves for the kiln.

Stoneware is usually made from several natural clays plus alumina and silica, to give it the desireable characteristics of plasticity, color, and the correct firing temperature. When fired, it becomes hard and vitreous, able to hold water without being glazed. It generally fires to a light gray but sometimes may be tan or even slightly reddish.

Earthenware is usually made from a natural clay and is low fired, as opposed to stoneware which is high fired, maturing at a kiln temperature between 1740° and 2130° F. The body is nonvitreous and will not hold a liquid unless glazed. The color after firing is usually buff or red, often quite dark. Earthenware is primarily used for industrial tiles, but some handsome tableware exists.

Porcelain is made from a prepared body containing kaolin, ball clay, feldspar, and flint. Hard, non-absorbant, of pristine whiteness, translucent in thin areas, it requires the highest fire of all pottery wares—up to 2670° F. Since it is not very plastic and requires more skill to work, it is not recommended as a clay body for beginning craftsmen.

A word about commercially produced dinnerware, generally known as "china": this is a whiteware body usually fired at a temperature higher than for earthenware but lower than for porcelain.

Although you can, in certain parts of the country, buy inexpensive earthenware bodies from brick and tile factories, these often contain coarse particles and other impurities which will cause trouble. Until you have more experience, it is recommended that you buy prepared clay bodies. See suppliers list page 95.

the firing process

Since the compounds which make up clay and glaze undergo many chemical changes during the firing cycle, this is a process that takes a certain amount of care. Unless you have purchased a kiln or are going to make the simple one described on page 87, you will, for awhile, probably give your pots to a professional to fire. Try to get as many pointers as possible from talking with him and watching him work. In this area, there is no substitute for actual experience. Depending upon the temperatures to which your kiln must be heated and *slowly* cooled, the firing cycle can take up to ten or even twelve hours. Firing to low earthenware temperatures should take eight hours, and never less than six. Pointers on firing a kiln are on page 86.

Oxidation firing is the normal firing in all types of kilns. The kiln you use will be heated either by electricity, gas, or oil. An electric kiln *always* has an oxidizing fire since there is no combustible fuel to consume the oxygen, which is always present. The results of oxidation are generally predictable, and you can obtain a wide range of bright and glossy colors with oxidation glazes. The common temperatures for oxidizing fire are under 2200° F.

Reduction firing is done during certain periods of the firing cycle in gas or oil kilns to develop the particular color characteristics of reduction glazes. After beginning with oxidizing fire, the burners and air intake are so regulated as to get incomplete combustion, which releases carbon into the kiln. This is known as reducing the atmosphere. Since carbon has a great affinity for oxygen, it will, in this atmosphere, steal it from the iron and copper oxides which are part of reduction glazes. When either of these are deprived of their oxygen, they remain suspended in glaze as pure colloidal metal. The normally green copper glaze then becomes a luscious ruby red, occasionally flecked with blues and purples, while iron oxide loses its usual brownish red color and takes on a variety of quiet gray-green tones. Reduction firing is best done at high temperatures—between 2200° F. and 2300° F. Although the range of colors available with reduction glazes is small, they more than make up for this with their subtlety and quiet beauty.

(Right) Subtle decoration achieved by salt beading built up on ridged surfaces. Salt-glazed pitcher by A. C. Garzio.

(Below) Reduction firing produced this rich, glossy glaze. Bowl by Lillian Samenfeld.

Salt glazing is a unique process in which raw clay pots are placed in a kiln and common table salt thrown in when the body is mature. At the completion of firing the pots are covered with a variegated brown and gray glaze. What happens here is that the salt combines with the silica in the body, usually stoneware, to form a handsome and particularly durable glaze. The process was discovered by German potters in the fifteenth century when they threw salt into the fire box of their wood-burning kilns. Salt glazing can be done today in downdraft open-fire kilns by throwing salt in through the opening around the burner or through special ports in the sides. Once a kiln is used for salt glazing, however, it is difficult to fire other kinds of ware in it with certainty; the interior of the kiln becomes coated with the glaze which is somewhat volatile. As your interest in the medium develops, you may come across a salt glazing kiln or decide to experiment with the technique in a workshop situation. The results will be well worth while. A point to remember: the interiors of salt-glazed pots have to be treated in the traditional fashion, that is, glazed before firing, as the salt vapors will not reach them.

CAUTION: A by-product of toxic chlorine gas is given off during the firing. Always be sure to fire in a well-ventilated area.

Raku is a process developed by Japanese potters and used by them for making tea ceremonial ware. The results are invariably distinctive. A pot made from a porous clay body is treated with low-fire lead glazes and placed in a red-hot kiln 1500°–1900° F. in a bisque state. When the glazes are smooth and shiny, the pot is removed with tongs and dropped into a bed of smoke-producing materials—wood chips, leaves, or straw. The smoke from these darkens any unglazed clay and causes local reduction in the glazed areas. After ten to fifteen minutes, the pot is plunged into cold water, and the process is complete. Instructions are found on page 90.

Oxidation firing of stoneware cookie jar created this iron-spotted effect. By Robert Turner.

Milky glaze is a typical result of Raku firing technique. By the author.

(Top) Wax resist with mat glaze slip decoration. Container with cover by Ralph Baccera. Photo by Sam Calder.

(Right) Coloring oxide adds strong design element to vase by Vivika and Otto Heino.

(Bottom left) White glaze slip with brushed decoration. Stoneware tea caddy by John Glick. Photo by Betty S. Wagner.

(Bottom center) Crackle glazed bottle by C. H. Brown. Photo Judith Gefter.

glaze

Glaze produces a layer of glass crystals on the clay surface. Its purpose is both decorative and, since it waterproofs a vessel, useful. Glaze is applied in a liquid state, and when the pot is fired it reacts and melts forming a thin layer of glass. There are low-fire glazes, those which melt at 1500° to 2000°F., and high-fire glazes, those which need temperatures of 2100° to 2300°F. (see page 92). Within these categories there are also many types: crackle, matte, crystalline, slip, luster, reduction, and salt glazes. The common procedure for glazing is first to bisque fire a pot—that is, fire it to a temperature of about 1750°F. A raw, dry clay vessel is fragile, and a bisque firing makes it hard enough to be handled safely yet porous enough to absorb glaze readily. For a beginner prepared glazes are recommended, but remember that specific glazes are designed for certain clays and kiln temperatures.

(Top right) Porcelain glazed bowl, 15″ diameter, by Ann Stockton. Photo by Ferdinand Boesch.

(Bottom left) Paddled porcelain bottle with crystalline glaze. By Herbert Sanders.

(Bottom Right) Slip trailing technique used to decorate bottle, by Tom McMillin. Courtesy of Craft Horizons.

the workshop

Although most beginning potters start with an absolute minimum of equipment—and this is certainly recommended—a growing interest in the medium will necessitate buying or making various items. The plan below, of an ideal studio for a professional potter, will help you plan ahead for the best use of available space. The important thing to keep in mind is the relationship of the setup to your own work procedure, such as the damp box and raw materials near the forming area or the kiln in a far corner of the studio. If you are handy with a saw, hammer, and nails, most of the plan below can be built rather than purchased. You can even build your own kiln (page 87), although it would have to be set up out of doors rather than in the workshop.

Floor plan of a workshop showing a logical work arrangement. Note that any arrangement to be convenient and efficient should apply to your work procedure.

1. Bench work and storage
2. Spray booth
3. Glaze and chemical storage
4. Storage—Cabinets and shelves
5. Kiln supplies
6. Kiln
7. Desk
8. Raw materials
9. Damp box
10. Sink
11. Wedging board
12. Potter's wheel
13. Tool storage
14. Finishing tables
15. Plaster table
16. Display cabinet

(Below) a sufficient number of shelves are necessary to store tools and materials, ware that is drying and waiting to be fired, and completed pieces.

materials and equipment

Basically the only items necessary for making pots with slabs and coils, aside from the kiln for firing, are clay and your hands, but there are a few tools which will be valuable. These are inexpensive and can be obtained from ceramics supply dealers or else improvised. Shown here, they are:

Ruler—Used for measuring or as a paddle for shaping work.

Chinese brush—Ideal for applying glaze. Small paint brushes of various sizes can also be used.

Wire trimming tool—For shaping and carving pots.

Pin (mounted on a handle)—Can be purchased, but a hat pin stuck through a cork will work as well.

Pencil—A tool for which you will find many uses.

Wire—For cutting through clay while wedging and slicing slabs (page 26–27). Attach a two-foot length to handles of some type—wood sticks, buttons, anything you can hold onto.

"Fettling" or potters knife—Best purchased, but a table knife or painter's palette knife will do.

As to the clay you will use, different types fire at different temperature, so it would be ideal to know in advance what kind of kiln will be available to you. Local potteries and Y.M.C.A.'s will often fire work for a small fee. If you don't know the kind of kiln you will be using, the best solution is to choose a clay with a wide firing range, one that can be used successfully at different temperatures. Look for one which will fire from 1900° to 2150° F.

Although most professional potters make their own glazes, I recommend that readers of this book buy prepared ones. These are again determined by your clay and the firing range of the kiln you are using, but an appealing variety is available to suit all requirements.

A list of major ceramic suppliers in the U.S.A., may be found on page 95. All have catalogs which describe their complete line. When buying in small amounts, try local building and supply dealers and craft shops.

Ruler

Potter's knife

Wire

Wire tool

Chinese Brush

Pencil

Pin

Wood modeling tool

Cutting the clay with the wire.

The kneading process.

Checking for air bubbles.

wedging

Raw clay, as it comes from a supplier, is full of air bubbles, and your first step will be to remove them. Even the smallest air pocket may cause the pot you have labored on to explode during firing, or, if your piece withstands the kiln air, a bubble may cause the fired clay to crack while it is cooling. There are two approaches to wedging which will give you clay of a smooth even texture, and I suggest that you try both to see which is most suitable for you.

The first approach is often called the "cut and slam" method. Take the lump of clay you are planning to work with and cut it in half, either by pushing it against a wedging wire stretched across your table-top or by holding a wire taut in your hands and pushing it through the clay. Throw one half down hard on the table; then throw the other half on top of the first. Cut and slam again and continue this procedure until all the air has been driven out of the clay. Your clay is "ready" when you can cut through it with a wire at any point and find it completely smooth.

The second approach is called "kneading." The clay is cut and thrown as above but then worked and pressed with your hands until smooth, much like working bread dough.

Overall, you will save time and energy by wedging a large amount of clay before you begin to work, so that you will not have to repeat the process for each pot. Store what you don't use immediately in a damp box (page 24) or any cool, damp place. Once clay is wedged, it stays wedged, so there is no danger of doing work which will have to be repeated.

You will now want to try your hand at making slabs and coils for the projects that follow. The only other basic process used in this book is making a rounded ball of clay for the "pinch" pot project on page 32. This is done simply by rolling a hunk of clay between your hands until it is fairly symmetrical.

making slabs

There are two ways of making slabs. In one, two guide sticks are placed, on a piece of burlap, as far apart as the slab is to be wide. The thickness of the sticks will determine the thickness of the slab, and I would suggest using sticks ½″ thick. Put a large ball of clay on the burlap between the sticks and roll it out with a rolling pin or dowel, resting whichever you use on the two pieces of lumber. This will give you slabs of an even thickness. Peel the clay off the burlap and trim the ragged edges. Although burlap is used so that clay won't stick to the table, it also gives one side of the slab an interesting texture. You might keep this in mind for later use.

The other method of making slabs is to take a big hunk of prepared clay and, on a table or a flat surface, pound it into a rectangle the size of a shoe box. Slabs can then be sliced off the squared piece of clay with a wire. Although this approach will not give you completely even slabs, it is much faster and is the method I prefer.

Either way, always give the slabs a chance to stiffen some before using them.

making coils

There are also two ways of making coils. For small, even ones roll out balls of clay on a freshly dampened table, so that the clay remains moist and does not break. Larger coils can be made by squeezing. Both methods are shown below.

Shaping clay ball for pinch project.

Rolling out small uniform coils.

Forming large uniform coils by squeezing.

Making slabs by rolling out clay.

Cutting slabs from clay block.

experimenting with texture

Before beginning to build clay forms of any kind, introduce yourself to the material in order to discover its possibilities as well as its limitations. The best way to go about this is to take a hunk of prepared clay in your hands and play with it. Squeeze it, bend it, pound it, pinch it. Fold or bend various thicknesses of it. Find out how far you can extend its plastic possibilities. For instance, does clay crack when you bend it? The more you handle your material in an exploratory way, the sooner answers to questions such as this will be second nature.

When you have spent some time in this meeting process take a big lump of clay and make it into a flat slab by pounding and slapping on a table or on the floor. You now have a surface on which to investigate what kinds of texture different objects

will make. Elementary as it may sound, when clay is in its plastic state, *anything* pressed on it can vary the surface. Take a look at the examples of textures on pages 16–17 as well as those on the opposite page and then use whatever comes to mind on the slab you have made: the prongs of a fork, the end of it, a spoon, bolts, a coin, a pencil, a knife blade. If you have access to professional ceramics tools, find out what these will do. Then remember that with your hands you can dig into clay, hit it, scratch it, brush it, gouge it. As stated above, anything and everything makes texture, but certain objects and methods produce more surface excitement than others.

Another method of patterning a slab of clay, one that will be used from time to time in the projects that follow, is to add coils or other pieces of clay to a surface, then paddle or beat them in with a stick. The effect is subtle and intriguing.

Almost any object can be used to impart texture to clay, and one tool can be used in different ways. Here a paddle etches ridges by digging and patting.

Dabbing with a brush, dotting with a finger nail, or making depressions with a sharp or blunt tool end are some examples of how to texture clay.

Textural decoration in sgraffito technique achieved by scratching out a design through a layer of applied slip. Bottle by Richard Peeler.

Motif made by applying small coils to rough surface.

making plaster stamps

Besides using "found objects," conventional pottery tools, and your hands to texture the surface of your work, simple stamps of your own design can be used to pattern the clay while still damp. This is a decorative device which dates back to pre-Christian times and probably began as a way of signing pots. Many potters today, in fact, use stamps in the form of a seal or signature to identify their work.

Stamps can be used singly or in combination, and there are a number of ways to make them. One of the more common is to carve a stamp out of wet clay. When fired, and therefore rock hard, it can be used to imprint fresh clay. Finer detail can be achieved in stamps carved out of plaster, how-

ever, and this is the method of stamp making described here.

The first step is to make small blocks of plaster. You can buy plaster in powdered form at any hardware or building supply store, but be sure to specify plaster of Paris or casting plaster. Sifting gently to prevent lumps, add one cup dry plaster to one cup of water. If possible, mix them in an old can which can be discarded when you are finished. When the mixture is lump free, pour it into small paper cups and let harden.

Two points to remember: be sure to add plaster to water, not water to plaster, and don't pour any of the mixture down a sink drain. It will harden and clog the pipes.

Pour plaster into paper cup.

Tear cup from hardened plaster.

Etch design in plaster.

Develop design of stamp.

Refine design.

Finished stamp and test impression.

When the plaster is solid, tear the paper off. You now have several blocks of uniform size. Sketch a variety of simple designs on them with a pin or pencil, then carve the plaster with a knife or an old umbrella spoke. Small wood carving tools also work well if you happen to have some. Plaster becomes harder the longer it sets, so it is a good idea to do the rough or major carving when it has just reached a solid state. Cleaning and sharpening of lines are best done after a few hours. As you are carving, stop from time to time and press the stamp into a piece of flat clay, so that you can see how the design is coming.

Stamped decoration used on bottles, 5″ high, by Paula Winokur. Photo by Robert Winokur.

The variety of plaster stamp designs range from fine detailed patterns for making delicate impressions, to bolder shapes to give more massive decoration on the clay.

An interesting tile can develop by a variety of stamps being impressed in the clay, as shown below.

the pinch pot

The pinch method is about the simplest way to make a pot. Since these pots are usually small and do not require tools in the actual forming, they offer to the beginner the best way of acquiring a feeling for the clay. Take advantage of this "getting acquainted" period before going to work on the slab and coil projects.

The idea is basic: a ball of wedged clay is pressed or pinched into a small shape. For this version, texturing is added at the end to make a small-scale vase. There are a number of ways you can use such pots, as containers for dried flowers or small fresh ones, as cigarette holders, or as catch-alls for paper clips and pins. I suggest that you follow the process through several times, working out as many different shapes as possible. When you get three or four that you really like, try out some of the methods you discovered while experimenting with texture earlier and see how they can be related to your pots. Just remember to keep your decoration to the scale of the pot. If you are making a vase which will hold fresh flowers, you will at least have to glaze the inside of the pot. Follow the instructions on pages 84–85. These pages will also tell you how to glaze the outside of the vase. As in all projects in this book, however, the emphasis is on forming methods and decoration with texture; the glaze treatments should be as straightforward as possible. After glazing, the vase is ready to be fired. If you have made a number of pinch pots, you can at this point take them to your local kiln. Do not arrive with one pot in hand, no matter how proud you might be of your work, for firing a single piece is costly and impractical.

Form a clay ball by slapping and rolling it in your hands. Rotate the ball in one hand while making an opening with the thumb of the other. Pinch the walls of the form to an even thickness all around and to the desired shape. By working slowly and pinching evenly as you work, a maximum of control can be achieved. Your hands should be kept dry while shaping. Avoid using water; it will tend to muddy and weaken the clay.

Completed small pinch pot with incised textured surface fired at cone 4 with a salt glaze.

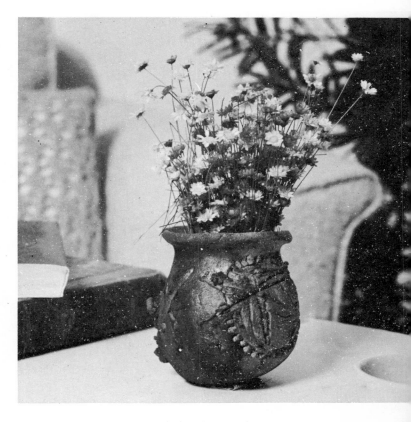

For a vase with a narrow top, fold the walls over themselves at intervals and continue pinching until walls are smooth and symmetrical. A light paddling with a ruler and smoothing with your fingers will help finish the form. A lip can be added by bending back the top of the walls. Texture the surface as you wish. A small stick was used to carve the design here. When the pot is finished, tap the bottom gently on the table to flatten.

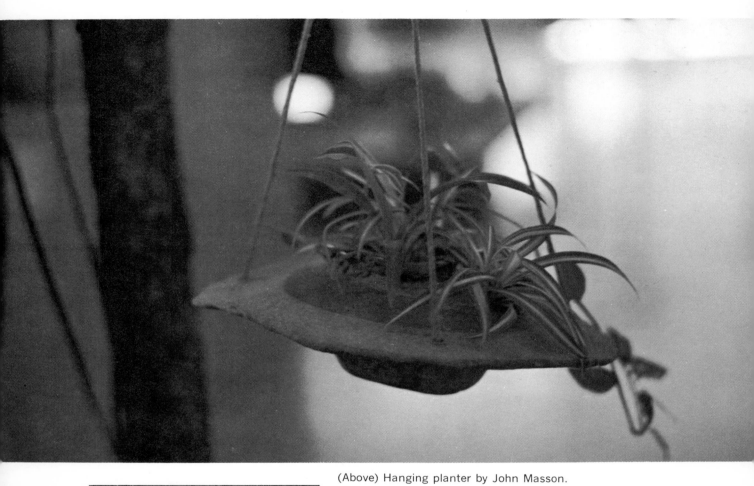

(Above) Hanging planter by John Masson.

(Left) Porcelain covered jar by Sema Charles.

(Below) Trays made by turning up slab edges.
By Toshiko Takaezu.

slab portfolio

Here are several examples of work done exclusively with slabs to show you the versatility of this technique before you start slab projects of your own. A tray can be made effectively by taking a slab and merely turning up the edges, or a simple weed vase by bending a slab into a cylindrical shape and boldly pinching the seam, as was done to make the pots in the photograph bottom right. The hanging planter, left, was made by pressing the center of a slab into a shallow mold, then when the clay hardened, holes were cut for the cords from which it hangs. The piece below left was done by joining seven small slabs. The variations are endless. The main thing to keep in mind is the character of the slab; don't try to make it look like something other than what it is. Also remember that it is ideal for surface effects and can often be enhanced by overall texture —achieved by making the slab on burlap or some other coarse material or surface.

(Top) Weed holders by author. See following page.

(Right) Slabs rolled into cylindrical shapes, pinched together, and added to wheel-thrown bases. By John Masson.

(Below) Multicolored pot by Sophia and John Fenton.

weed holders

A SIMPLE SLAB PROJECT.

No matter what part of the country you live in, there are many kinds of fascinating weeds or wild flowers which you might like to display, and in this slab project you can make a weed holder which can be hung on the wall. Aside from the weeds or flowers themselves, the interest here will come from the way you treat the surface of the slab, using the techniques set forth in the section on "Experimenting with Texture" (pages 28–29). Since the holders are quick and easy to make, try doing several, so that you can group them in an arrangement. This same design could also be used to make pencil holders.

Weed holder with burlap impression ready for glazing and firing.

Roll out clay on burlap and cut a slab approximately 8″ x 5″ and two strips about 1″ x 5″ and ½″ x 2½″. Lay the larger strip near the bottom of the slab and the other at top center so that the two ends are on the slab and the rest hangs over the edge.

Join strips to slab base by beating them lightly with a paddle. With a pencil make several indentations in the bottom strip. Punch a hole through the top strip. The slab will hang by this on a nail or hook. Let the holder dry, then glaze and fire.

trivets

A SIMPLE SLAB PROJECT USING PLASTER STAMPS. This is a slab project that is almost foolproof for the beginner. In fact this one, which utilizes the carved plaster stamps made earlier (pages 30–31), would be a welcome gift glazed in colors to match the decoration of a friend's kitchen, breakfast room, or patio. If you have made several plaster stamps, as was suggested, they can be used singly or in combination, and the impressions can be scattered or used as an overall design. A hot plate usually holds a pot or casserole with a flat bottom, so it is a good idea, when you are finished, to paddle the tile lightly to insure a level surface.

For two trivets cut one slab—this will be cut in half later. Have slab slightly larger than the sizes you want both trivets to be since it will not hold its shape during stamping and will have to be trimmed afterward. Press a design with a stamp. Trim outer edges and divide slab in two, then paddle. Dry, then glaze and fire.

Roll out two slabs on a coarse material, such as burlap, and cut to approximately 10″ X 8″ and 5″ X 5″. Bend the larger slab into a cylinder and join its sides by pressing one into the other with your thumb. Trim one end of cylinder and place it, trimmed end down, on second slab. Cut excess clay from base to align with cylinder.

Turn cylinder, with base upside down, and with your fingers join base to the sides. Right the cylinder so that it rests on base and join interior seams, then trim top of pot.

cylindrical vase

CREATING A CYLINDRICAL FORM USING SLABS.

This project gives you the opportunity to use a slab with an overall texture; as described in the section on forming slabs (page 27). Although a cylindrical vase such as this can be any height, the one here is about 7″ tall, perfect for many short-stemmed flowers. Because of the overall texture and the additional stamping and carving, the rich surface of this pot would look very well in unglazed clay, but the interior would have to be treated since the vase must hold water. In the example shown, the stamping and carving were combined in one area, but you can make other designs; the variations are endless and are limited only by your imagination. NOTE: make the slab at least ½″ thick so that it will not crack when you bend it into a cylinder.

Completed vase fired at cone 4; the inside is entirely glazed so that the vase can hold water.

Retouch textured areas made smooth during handling by pressing a piece of burlap into the clay. Decorate with stamp and carving, or in a different manner if you prefer. When the pot is dry, it is ready for glazing and firing.

ideas for the slab method

Of all the hand-building techniques, the slab method is the most versatile and offers the most opportunities for creative exploration. Before continuing to other planned slab projects, here are a few illustrations of work done with this technique to help you with ideas of your own. As you can see in photographs on both pages, craftsmen have used the slab method with flare and originality for screens or room dividers. Particular notice should be taken of the wind chime at right with whimsical faces incised in free-form slabs; this could not be done as effectively in any other technique. The unglazed stoneware, is an appropriate example of the versatility of the slab. The crèche from Mexico, at the top of the opposite page, was made by folk artisans who used slabs for the manger, painting them with dark brown slip, then freely modeling the figures inside. The wall mural below right was made of several slabs with applications of other slab forms and freely modeled shapes; the work was then glazed. Since most clay, particularly glazed high-fire ware, is able to withstand the elements, it is possible to make projects for both indoor and outdoor use. Tiles which can be cemented into a kitchen, bath, or patio are still another approach to this process.

(Left) Room divider or screen made with varied shaped tiles and strung vertically in open wood frame panels, size 4' x 8'. By Henry Lin. Courtesy of Craft Horizons.

(Below) Hanging free form planter made with slabs, unglazed, by Robert Winokur. Courtesy of the American Craftsmen's Council.

(Above) Sculptured forms shaped from coils combined with slabs to create this Mexican creche.

(Right) Wind chime made by stringing small decorated circular slabs together and hanging from a wooden bar. By Robert and Paula Winokur.

(Below) Ceramic wall relief. After piece is developed, it is cut into squares to fit into kiln for firing, then reassembled. Size 24″ × 38″. By Henry Lin.

Using the technique described on page 27, with a wire cut six slabs from a rectangle of wedged clay, each about 5″ × 10″ and ½″ thick. Let slabs set, then score edges that will be joined in making the four sides of pot, scratching them with a pin tool or a fork.

Before assembling slabs add soft clay or slip (see glossary) to the scored edges. Join the edges of two slabs and work them together with a modeling tool.

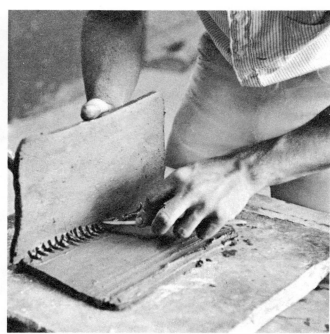

covered jar

RECTANGULAR SHAPES

The purpose of this project is to give you the experience of making a four sided piece with handles and cover. An additional point of interest here is pinching method of sealing the joins. Besides serving to cement the sides, this method adds a decorative quality.

After you have made the slabs necessary for the jar, let the clay dry until it is stiff but still wet enough so that you can pinch it. If you don't allow the slabs to stiffen, they may collapse during construction of the project. This applies to all slab work. Another general rule is to make all joins inside a slab pot as strong as possible by scoring and adding bits of fresh clay. That is, make scratches across the joining areas with your pin-on-stick tool or more practically, a fork. Then add bits of clay to the scored areas and push them into the scratches, smoothing over the seam with your fingers. Since the finishing of a slab pot usually cannot be done until the clay is very stiff (but not leather-hard), you may like to work on more than one piece at a time.

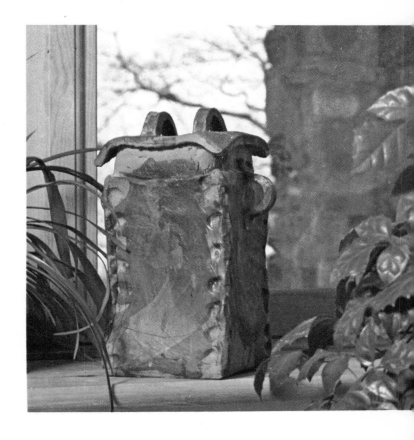

Add the third slab in the same manner. If desired, an even stronger join can be achieved by laying a coil of clay along the seam and working it in. Add fourth slab. This must be stiffer than the others to support itself during application.

Continued on next page

Covered jar—continued from previous page

Turn four sides upright and place on another slab which will be the base. Cut off excess clay and join the base on the inside. You can pinch the outer seams of the pot together to strengthen the construction and to decorate.

To make the cover, cut a piece of clay 6″ square and attach a strip of clay, the same size as the handles, to the center of it. When this slab is placed on top of the jar, it will adjust to the contour of the neck.

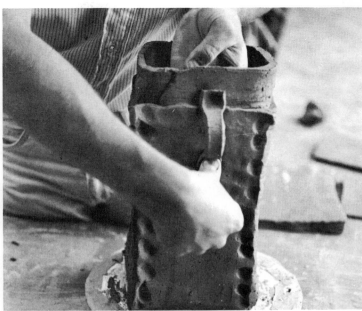

Cut a piece of clay about 2″ × 8″ and wrap it around the top of the jar to form the neck. Work it in with a fettling knife, again from the inside. Cut two strips of clay for handles and attach these to the sides of the jar, top ends first, using the fettling tool and your fingers to join them to the form.

Trim the cover slab so that it is in proportion to the jar. Allow jar to dry thoroughly, then glaze and fire. Do not keep the cover on the pot while drying or firing.

Cut three slabs, each approximately 6″ X 12″, for the sides of the lantern. Score the upper sides along the 12″ edges, then spread slip on all scored areas. Put one slab flat and attach the scored edge of another slab to it and work edges together with a fettling tool on the inside where they join. Smooth the outside join with your finger so that it will be strong enough to hold the slabs at a right angle. Join the remaining slab in the same manner.

Bend the upright slabs together to form a triangle, joining the upper seam by pinching the clay. Turn upright and pat all edges until smooth with a ruler or a small piece of wood. Let clay stiffen for a while, then sketch a design on the sides.

garden lantern

TRIANGULAR SHAPES

This slab-built lantern constructed of three sides was designed for outdoor use, but it would also be effective indoors among an arrangement of house plants or suspended with several other slab lanterns, each of a slightly different size. The lantern is designed to be illuminated either with a small electric light bulb or with a candle, and you should choose which you will use before starting the project. If electrified, the bulb will be at the top, if the lantern is suspended, or at the bottom, if it is self-supporting. Also, while you enjoy seeing a candle through the cutouts in the sides, it is more aesthetically pleasing if an electric bulb is concealed by lining the inside with rice paper. Although the lantern we will make here is triangular, round or square-sided ones can be made using the same general approach. This is another project that would look well unglazed, but if you decide to give it color, remember that the cutout designs are the strongest element.

When the clay is leather hard, cut out the designs. Trim the top of lantern so that it is even and cut a top for it from another slab. Score all edges of the cover and the top of lantern. Lightly paddle the cover into place. If the lantern is going to be suspended, you will need a hole for a cord made from a small slab of clay.

Smoothed coils with stamp decoration. By S. Elliot Sayles.

Open coil construction by Rose Krebs.

Coils worked in with modeling tool. By Ellen King.

Wheel-thrown pot combined with coils, unglazed. By Karen Karnes.

Hand-built with smoothed coils, slip decoration. By Frances Simches.

coil portfolio

The building of coil upon coil was the way primitive man made his pots, and it was this easy method of gradual building that eventually suggested the wheel. At one period, coil work was done in a production-line manner with one man sitting at a turntable on the ground, rotating it and laying on a rope of coil which another craftsman would make and feed to him over his shoulder. The man at the turntable soon learned that if water and pressure were used when the turntable was rotated, the walls of a pot would rise and become thinner. Potters later discovered from using the turntable that clay could be made to rise without the use of coils. With speed, water, and the proper handling, clay could be thrown and pulled up. Thus, the potter's wheel evolved, and production became much faster. Because of the feeling of structure which you can get with coils, the next few projects will give you work different in feeling from the slab exercises. The coil itself can be allowed to show or it can be smoothed over.

(Right) Large patio bottle with coils partially smoothed. By the author.

(Below left) Coil built vase, partially smoothed to achieve ridged effect. By Frances Simches.

(Below right) Coil built pot that has coils worked in for scalloped pattern. By S. Elliot Sayles.

Pat out a small slab of clay about the size of the palm of your hand. Cut a circle from it, about 3″ in diameter and ⅜″ thick. Remove the excess clay. Circle this base with a series of coils to form the walls of the pitcher. As you work, join the coils on the inside of the pot with a modeling tool.

Direct the coils outward at the top to make a spout. For the handle take three 12″ coils, braid them and flatten with a ruler or small stick.

cream pitcher

SMALL COIL

Your introduction to coil work is a small pitcher which openly displays the technique used. Small coils will be used for this project since they are easier for the beginner to manipulate. The pitcher will only be six or seven inches high and will be rolled rather than pinched into shape. For one pitcher you will need up to twelve coils, each approximately twelve inches long, but I suggest that you make twice this number and work on two pitchers simultaneously. During coiling, one pitcher may begin to weaken, and you will have to stop and let it stiffen for a while before beginning again. As was illustrated previously, to make coils roll out balls of clay on a slightly damp board, working with both hands from the center outward. A damp board is particularly necessary when making small coils since it prevents them from drying out and breaking. Cover the finished coils with a damp cloth. The pitcher will have to be glazed on the inside, whether you are going to use it at the table or as a small vase. The outside need not.

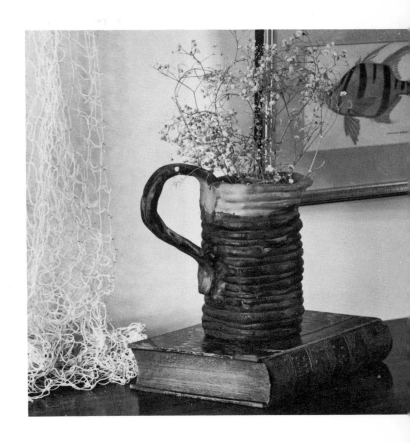

Attach the handle directly behind the spout by smoothing the clay to the coiled body of the pitcher. The pot is now ready to be dried, glazed, and fired.

Roll out a lump of clay into a circular shape, about 12″ in diameter. Cut into an even circle. As you work along, squeeze out large, snake-like ropes of clay about 1″ thick. Build the bottle by winding these clay ropes around the circular base.

After each coil is added, pinch it securely to the previous one. Score all coils on the inside to make a good join all around. If you find it necessary to interrupt your work, be sure to deeply score the top of the pot before you begin again.

patio bottle

LARGE COIL

Coils can be used on a wheel-built pot to increase its size—a pot is thrown to its maximum height, large coils are joined on and built up to make the pot larger—but exclusive use of coils is the best way of making the bottle of this project. This is by far the largest work presented in this book, and from my teaching experience one of the most exciting as it gives the beginner a chance to make something of size and scope. However, since the piece is about three feet tall, make sure that you have a large enough kiln available to fire it. If you don't have a kiln large enough, adapt the project to the size that is available to you. If you like, you can take several days to finish the bottle, covering the top with a sheet of plastic each time you stop. The base will then be able to dry out while the upper part remains damp and workable.

When the desired height is reached, cut a slab strip large enough for two handles, about 2½″ wide, 8″ long, and ½″ thick, and shape to bottle. Add rim of 1″ thick clay and smooth by patting with a stick. Since this is a large piece, it will take longer to dry before being glazed and fired.

Cut a 5″ circle from a slab of clay and make two holes in its center; this will be for the light bulb cord or any other support. Roll out at least a dozen small coils, about 12″ long, and cover them with a damp cloth. Circle three rows of coils around the slab, scoring them to the base on the inside for a firm join.

With the other coils, build up the form until it is about 8″ high. Experiment and arrange coils to your own design. Score the coils on the inside where they touch. Let the clay stiffen for a while, then turn the piece upside down.

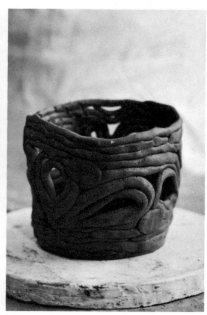

hanging lamp

FREE FORM COILS

In the first two coil projects, the construction was relatively pre-planned—that is, you built up coils in circles until a form was completed. This hanging lamp, on the other hand, gives you freedom to use your ingenuity. As you can see from the photographs, coils are snaked around, back and forth on top of themselves, rather than round and round, to build the lamp. This is a project I have given my classes at The Brooklyn Museum Art School in New York, and the students have usually had more fun with it than any other. Whatever you do, don't try to follow exactly the example shown. Do whatever your imagination dictates. If you don't like what is happening, wad the clay up and begin again. This is one of the great virtues of clay: it is cheap, and you don't have to be overly cautious with it. As to finishing the lamp, an all-over glaze in one of the many earth colors could work very well, particularly since you might want to hang it in a corner of your yard. If used indoors, the convoluted shapes of the coils make intriguing patterns on the walls around it.

Add more coils to the top, allowing them to stand about 3″ high. This is the way the lamp will hang after it has dried, been glazed, and fired.

Select a bowl whose shape you like, coat the inside with vaseline or cooking oil, and pour in enough plaster to duplicate form. (See pages 30–31 for directions on mixing plaster.) Let the plaster harden, then separate from the bowl.

a simple bowl

PRESS MOLD

One of the most direct ways of duplicating a shape is by the press mold method. The bowl shown here or a series of bowls which are made with this technique can be either glazed or unglazed; however, here is a good opportunity to try your hand at some simple brushwork (see pages 88–89). This bowl can also serve as the point of departure for future pots, acting as a base to which coils or slabs can be added. By adding a coil-built stem, it could easily become a compote. Although the instructions are for a plaster mold, one of clay could work just as well.

NOTE: whenever using a clay mold, place a piece of burlap or cloth on it before laying on the slab of fresh clay, or the two will stick together.

With mold inverted, press a clay slab onto it. Cut away the excess and smooth. Make a ring with a coil of clay for the foot of the bowl. Paddle the foot until you have an even surface, then score. (Leave the bowl on the mold for about twenty minutes so that it hardens some but does not dry completely, for clay shrinks when drying, and the pressure from the plaster will make it crack.) Remove from mold, dry completely, then glaze and fire.

press mold hot plate

A press mold can be made in two ways: a shape can be hollowed out from a plaster slab by carving, or a form can be built up with clay, then covered with a layer of poured plaster. Once the plaster has set, the clay is removed. Remember that in either method you are making a negative pattern, and that the depressions you carve will be projections in the positive pattern. A simple geometric design is recommended for the beginner.

Take handfuls of clay and press them firmly into the mold. Make a bottom layer so that you can feel the clay going into the depressions of the mold. Then fill in with more clay until the level is slightly higher than the surface of the mold. With a ruler or stick, level the clay so that it is even with the top of the mold. Let the clay harden for a short time, then lift it gently from the plaster. Allow to dry, then glaze and fire.

A slip casting mold is made of plaster and comes in two parts which lock together. It has a cavity for the slip to collect and harden. Place the two halves of the mold together and pour slip into the channels leading to the inside space. Allow slip to set for at least fifteen minutes.

Remove the top half of mold, exposing the plate. With a fettling knife trim off the extra clay where the slip was poured through the channels.

dinner plates

SLIP CASTING

If you feel you would like to make a set of dinner plates, you would find it a difficult task with only slab and coil techniques at your disposal. I suggest that for this purpose you look into the many slip casting molds that are available through the suppliers on page 95, and then buy the one which makes a shape that pleases you most. You can decorate each of the plates individually if you wish. However, limit the decoration on them to glazing as any texturing other than a light stroke around the outer edge will only catch food as well as make cutting on the plate impossible. Since you will be using slip for these plates, you can finish the plates with any of the various stoneware glazes. Striking abstract designs can be done by brushing, pouring, and even splattering glazes of two or three colors. It doesn't matter if they make a pool in the center. When the plates come out of the kiln, the glazes will have fused to form a smooth, glossy surface, and the depth of color will be really impressive.

Lift the finished plate from the mold and texture it in any manner you choose. The edges of this plate were not smoothed in order to retain a hand made look. Let dry thoroughly before glazing and firing. Although this method insures uniformity in duplication, subtle differences can occur which will add individuality and interest to the total set.

To make three cups, begin with a plaster cup mold and three slabs of clay about ½″ thick, cut slightly wider than the mold is high. Wrap one of the slabs around the mold, pressing it together at the seam and then all over to make an even shell.

Trim off the excess clay at the top. Remove the mold and let the clay harden for at least fifteen minutes. Repeat process for each mug.

set of mugs

PRESS MOLD

In this variation of the press mold, a set of mugs is quickly made by wrapping slabs of clay around a cylindrical form. The form is again a plaster mold, this time made by pouring plaster of Paris into a paper cup (of the size desired) and, letting it harden. (Refer to the directions for mixing plaster of Paris in the section on plaster stamps, pages 30–31). Once the cup has been made, take some care in smoothing the inside so that it can be washed easily. The outsides can be finished with glaze and/or texture. Since you are making a set, invent a theme for the decoration even though each piece will be a variation. This is one of the most practical projects in this book and one which you may return to often. As was suggested with the slab trivets, a set of these mugs would make an excellent gift.

Cut strips for handles about 1″ X 4″, or slightly larger than desired. (clay will shrink during drying and firing). Add handle to cup by pressing ends, top first, then proceed with decoration. In mugs shown above a scored coil was wrapped around the upper part of each.

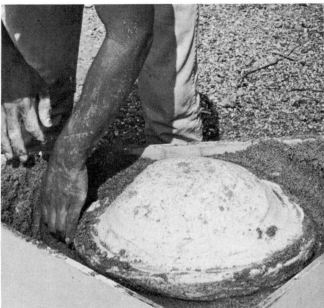

Build up a form with wet sand and texture the surface with a blunt tool. Keep the sand damp so that the form will not crumble. Dig the sand away from the base and carefully pour a thin layer of plaster over the form. If you are working on the beach, remember that FRESH WATER must be used to make the plaster. When this plaster has set a bit, pour on another thin layer. Repeat until shell is about 3″ thick. When hard, remove and allow to dry for about a week. If the model remains on the beach, cover at night with a sheet of plastic.

When the plaster is completely dry, line the inside with a slab of clay, pressing it onto the irregular surface. Patch areas with additional clay where necessary. Completed shell should be about ½″ thick.

weed pot

SAND CASTING

The mold technique that is presented here is probably the most fun, since it uses sand and gives you a chance to work outdoors. If you live near the ocean, beach sand is ideal. If you don't, the kind you buy at a hardware store will do just as well. The technique we are using is called sand casting, and the result is a fairly large, strongly textured weed pot. Not only does this process allow you to repeat the object, but it gives you a large-size pot with an entirely different quality than that of coiling or slab-building. You begin by modeling one half of a pot form about 12″ to 18″ long in wet sand. This design is then coated with plaster, which forms the mold. After the mold has hardened, two clay shells are made in it, for the two halves, which are then joined to make the body of the pot. The process could also be used to make one-piece castings, such as bird baths, and platters.

Grains of sand lining the shell will create texture. When the clay has dried in the mold for about twenty minutes, remove and let stiffen. Repeat process. Join the two halves by scoring their edges and adding slip before pressing together. Hold for a few minutes until the slip starts to dry. Add a thick coil of clay for a base. Cut a hole in the top of the bottle and add a thick coil of clay for a neck, pressing it firmly to the body of the bottle. Dry, then glaze and fire.

(Above) Vase built up with slabs on a wheel-thrown base. By Len Stack.

(Right) Slab cylindrical bottles with thrown tops and bases by John Masson.

(Below) Thrown and slab covered jar by Bob Arneson.

combined methods portfolio

Once you have learned the basic techniques of hand-built pottery, you can expand the possibilities of these methods by combining or using them together—coil with slab, slab with mold, coil with mold, or coil with slab and mold. The play of one type of construction against another gives exciting contrasts of form and surface which are not available with one technique alone; later on, when you have learned how to throw on the wheel, you will find the combination of thrown and hand-built methods particularly exciting. The pots at the right, for example, were made by throwing cylindrical forms, then wrapping slabs around them, and paddling them onto the thrown shapes. The pots at the left were constructed by bending and pinching slabs into tall cylinder shapes, then adding wheel-thrown necks and bases. The next projects will show you ways to combine the approaches demonstrated thus far. While working, think of some other pots that you could make with slab, coil, and mold methods. When you have a good idea, make a note of it or sketch it for future use. The examples on these pages only hint at the possibilities.

(Top right) Flasks by Dennis Parks and (below) bottle and vase by Winifred M. Holt.

Prepare a slab of wedged clay, about 10″ × 5″, several small coils, and a plaster stamp. You will also need the pin tool. Stamp a design on the slab. Trim the long sides so that the slab curves in, or leave it as a rectangle. With your hand under the center, lift the slab so that it falls into an arc.

Take one of the coils and circle it into a cylinder just wider than the base of a candle. Remember that clay shrinks when it dries. Attach cylinder to the slab by scoring its base. Smooth the join, or leave the score marks as is for a decorative effect. Prepare two short coil cylinders for the sides. Cut at an angle to fit the slope of the slab base. Then attach.

candle holder

SLAB, COIL, WITH PLASTER STAMP.

Two basic techniques and a decorative device-slab, coil, and the plaster stamp—are combined to make an arc-shaped candle holder. This is another project which lends itself to many variations, and feel free to make your own adaptations. As you begin to master many of the basic principles of pottery you no doubt will have more confidence in your abilities to work out original designs. A series of candle holders following the basic plan could be made, with different stamps used on each as well as different placement of the coil holders. And the base slab does not have to curve in. It could remain a rectangle or take the form of a gentle S-shape. Since this is not a time-consuming project, play around with it before deciding on a piece, or pieces, to be glazed and fired. Don't labor too hard on any one; the more spontaneous your approach, the better the result.

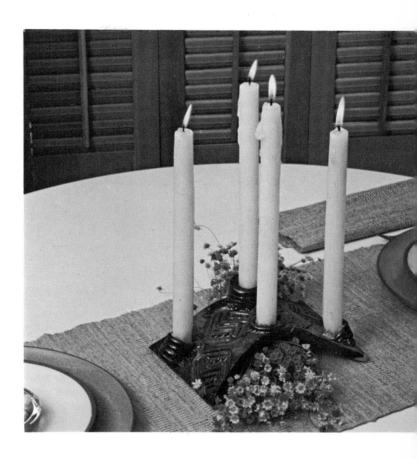

Make another coil cylinder for the top and attach. The piece when dry is ready to be glazed and fired.

Prepare three slabs, each 4″ × 8″ and roll out six coils at least 12″ long. Have ready on your work table a plaster stamp, a ruler or paddle, a fettling knife, and a pin tool. With the stamp, make a row of impressions down the center of one slab. From another slab cut a circle about 4″ in diameter for the base of the vase. Cut a 3″ strip lengthwise from the third slab and wrap it around the base. Score inside and pinch on the outside to secure firmly. With the coils, build up the wall of the pot, circling them around two or three times. Score the coils on the inside to each other and to the slab.

Trim the stamped slab, leaving narrow margins on either side of the impressed design, and add it onto the coils, again joining on the inside. Take the leftover 1″ strip and set it onto the inside rim of the stamped slab, so that the entire thickness of the stamped slab protrudes. Join and score.

small vase

SLAB, COIL, WITH PLASTER STAMP

This vase, an example of the combined method
technique, is a cylindrical form, partially glazed,
with handles, using the slab, coil and plaster stamp.
I suggest that you go through the project once as
is and then work out your own version. Unless you
are using a high-fire stoneware body, if the vase is
to hold water at least the inside will have to be
glazed. Some glaze on the exterior might be effective,
but I advise caution for the construction is the pot's
own decoration.

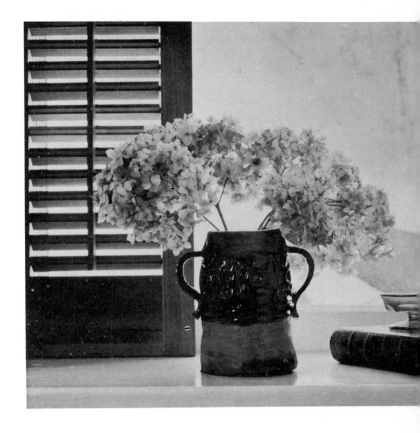

From the remaining clay, cut two strips, 4″ × 1″, for the handles and apply them to the form, upper
ends first. Smooth the vase to the point of refinement you want, but don't overwork. Dry, glaze,
and fire.

Prepare five slabs each about 6″ × 10″ and ¼″ to ½″ thick. Also have a simple bowl-shape mold (see page 56) for the base and press one of the slabs over it.

Trim the excess clay and add foot rim, as on page 56. Let stiffen for about twenty minutes, then remove it from the mold.

teapot

SLAB AND PRESS MOLD

Mold and slab techniques are used to make a teapot which is functional and decorative. There are several things to keep in mind here. If you want to brew loose tea leaves in the pot, do not cut a hole for the spout as directed, but instead make a series of small holes. You must be careful, however, that they do not later become plugged with glaze. The position of the spout is also important. Its point must be at a level near the top of the pot, and its base should not be too low, or the teapot will hold very little liquid. The thinner you make your slabs for this project the better, as you do not want the pot to be too heavy when filled. If possible, make this project with a stoneware body. But no matter what clay you use, be sure the teapot is at room temperature or has been slightly warmed before pouring boiling water into it. You can probably find a bamboo handle similar to the one I have used at any of the many shops specializing in items from the Orient.

To build the sides, cut a 5″ strip from one of the slabs, long enough to fit around the form. Cut a second strip of clay 4″ wide and place it just within the diameter of the first. Place it on top; join and score all seams.

Continued on next page

Teapot—continued from previous page

Join by scoring and smoothing the clay on the inside and working the two sections together on the outside with your finger. From one of the slabs make a cylinder which will be the spout of the teapot.

Cut two strips of clay about 3″ × ½″ for the lugs. The bamboo handle will be attached to these after firing. Join them to the teapot, upper ends first.

Place the spout on the side of the pot, and, with a pencil, mark where it will join. Within this area make either several holes, or one hole which will correspond with the inside diameter of the spout. Join spout to teapot and smooth seam.

For the cover, cut a 5″ × 5″ slab and a strip of clay the same size as the lugs. Shape handle to the top of the slab. Place the cover on top of the pot and bend the corners down so that it fits comfortably. If it is too large, trim to fit. After teapot is thoroughly dry, glaze and fire, then attach bamboo handle to lugs. Remember to remove cover during drying and firing.

Egyptian paste jewelry

This interesting and intriguing process was handed down from ancient times. It is necessary here to use Egyptian paste that is commercially purchased or that is made from the formula given.

The name Egyptian paste comes from a combination of clay and glaze that the ancients used for their distinctive ceramic beads. Modern potters have not, to my knowledge, been able to duplicate the Egyptian formula, but we have come up with something quite similar. Although it feels like and can be worked the same as ordinary clay—rolled in balls, pinched into squares, patted into slabs and cut—it eliminates half the steps since glaze is already part of the clay body.

Rolling paste into coils.

Coils cut into small pieces and shaped, with a hole ⅛″ diameter, bored in each, for stringing.

Paste beads ready for firing.

There are two formulas for Egyptian paste. One fires with a dry matte finish, and the beads can be fired together in a bowl without sticking. Both formulas, however, only require one firing to arrive at the finished result. The second formula gives a jewelry that has a glossy, glaze-like finish. Beads made with this formula must be strung on nichrome wire rather than placed inside pots when fired.

Below are formulas for both versions, as well as the various colorants which can be added. The ingredients can be purchased from the ceramic suppliers listed on page 95. You need only mix them with water until you have a clay-like substance.

EGYPTIAN PASTE FORMULAS—Cone 06–04

Dry—Beads will not stick together when fired.

MATT BASE

Silica	75 grams
Copper carbonate	2
Sodium bicarbonate	2
Bentonite	8
Frit, lead	20

Shiny—Beads must be strung on nichrome wire when fired:

GLOSS BASE

Oxford spar	800 grams
Flint	400
China clay	500
Ball clay	100
Sodium bicarbonate	120
Soda ash	120
Whiting	100
Fine white sand	160

COLORANTS—FOR BOTH FORMULAS

Green	3% Chrome
Turquoise	3% Black copper oxide
Blue	1%—3% Cobalt carbonate
Black	3% Manganese dioxide
Brown	3% Red iron oxide

(Above) Necklace of pre-colored Egyptian paste combined with grapefruit seeds. By Frances Schneider.

(Top right) Detail of necklace, unglazed, by Frances Schneider.

(Middle right) Detail of necklace, pre-colored Egyptian paste with incised designs. By Susan Mauss.

(Right) Bracelet, pins, and earrings by Susan Mauss.

Wheel head 10″ to 12″ in diameter

Seat

Bench

Bearing

Shaft

Foot brace and rest

40″

35″

Fly wheel

32⅝″

Bearing

14½″

34″

36½″

Home-built workbench and kick wheel with dimensions.

the potter's wheel

If you have a way with a hammer and saw, you can save more than half on costs by building your own kick wheel frame. Specifications may be obtained from your dealer.

The dimensions, such as the height of the bench or the distance between table and bench, can be varied to assure your comfort at the wheel.

For the wheel assembly, you can purchase from certain ceramic supply companies a kit containing the wheel assembly. Components of the kick wheel consist of a 12″ diameter throwing head, usually marked with concentric circles, and a steel shaft

with bearing movement which connects the throwing head with the balance wheel, weighing approximately 100 pounds.

Coordinated foot movements on the wheel control starting, speeds in the throwing, and stopping.

Since the method of throwing ceramics on the potter's wheel is the major forming process used by the professional, the reader will want to be as familiar with it as possible and with the terminology used. Not only is throwing the most popular approach to pottery, but it is also the most difficult to master. As stated in the introduction to forming methods, this is an aspect of the medium that you should learn with an instructor. The going may be tough at first, but there is nothing quite comparable to the thrill of seeing clay grow quickly from a hunk thrown on the center of the potter's wheel to a full, voluminous form.

References to the potter's wheel are found in the earliest hieroglyphic records of the ancient Egyptians, and although there are many types today, none differ much from the first one made 6000 years ago. Potters in the Far East and Middle East use models which are sunk into the ground, and the craftsman squats over it as he throws. Western ceramists use models made so that one sits or stands while throwing. In this country we have both kick wheels and electric wheels. The kick wheel is the direct descendant of the one used by primitive man and is the more popular of the two since control over speed is easily maintained by the foot while the hands are kept on the work.

There are also some good electric wheels on the market, but with them the potter does not have as much control over his work. Although the kind you eventually use will be a matter of personal preference, I believe that one should learn to throw on a kick wheel. On the opposite page, are plans for a simple model which you can build and use at home.

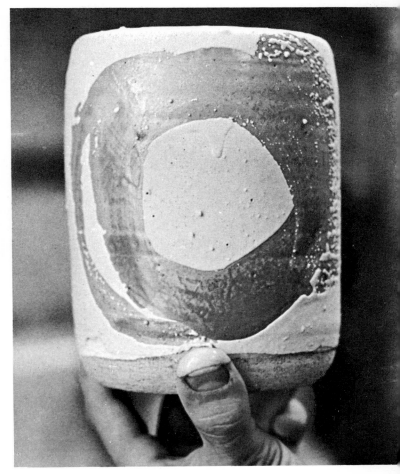

A cylindrical form. This is the basic shape for all wheel-thrown pieces.

Cross section of a cylindrical form showing the different stages of development as it is being built on the wheel.

Porcelain plates by Sema Charles.

Stoneware bottle, partially glazed, by Ellen King.

Bottles textured by slip trailing. By John Glick.

OPPOSITE PAGE

(Top right) Combination of two pieces, cylinder and base, thrown separately and joined after stiffening. Vase by Bob Arneson.

(Bottom left) Bottle, flattened after it was thrown to achieve oval shape, by Len Stack.

(Bottom right) Bowl with brushed decoration by Ralph Bacerra.

wheel portfolio

The examples of ceramics shown here were done on the potter's wheel, and on the following pages are step-by-step photographs that take you through the action of throwing a cylindrical pot. One of the main differences from slab and coil work offered by the wheel is absolute *symmetry*—although a pot can be given a lop-sided effect or be distorted in a number of ways once it has been taken from the wheel (page 83). The clay must be centered, and as the wheel makes several revolutions per second the slightest manipulation with your hands makes an identical change over the entire circumference. Volume is also a consideration in wheel thrown pots and thrown shapes are as interesting for their outer appearance as for the space they contain. This interplay of inner and outer form is also more peculiar to wheel pots than to those done with slab and coil.

To demonstrate the process of wheel throwing, on the following pages the cylinder is used as the basis for all thrown shapes whether a bottle, a plate, or a bowl. A cylinder can, of course, take a range of forms—low and wide as for a bowl, or tall and narrow as for the bottle shape presented here.

wheel throwing

Clay should be perfectly wedged so that it has no bubbles or lumps, and it must be neither too hard nor too soft. Place a ball of prepared clay directly on the wheel or on a moistened bat which is centered on the wheel. Set the wheel in motion and with pressure from the hands work the clay ball to the exact center of the wheel.

Whenever possible join the hands for better control over the clay. Since cylinders tend to flare out, they must be closed in often by "necking"—a technique that causes walls to thicken and rise.

Once the ball of clay has been centered perfectly, open it out with your thumbs. With very little pressure pull the clay up so that it rises into a cylinder.

More upward pressure will give a larger cylinder with thinner walls. The uneven top can be cut off with a pin tool.

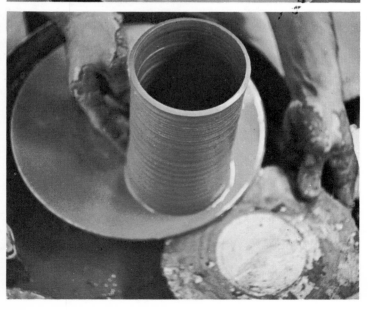

(Top) A wooden modeling tool or pencil is used to trim the excess clay from the base of the finished cylinder.

(Center) To remove the pot from the wheel, hold a wire taut and push it under the base through to yourself. If the pot was thrown on a bat, unfasten the bat from the center of the wheel and remove with the pot. In this way, the work will not have to be handled until dry.

(Bottom) After the pot has been removed from the wheel with a wire, slide it gently off onto a board or plaster bat and allow to dry.

variations

WHEEL-THROWN FORMS

The classical shape of a perfectly symmetrical pot thrown on the wheel is only one aspect of the modern ceramist's achievement. Often the modern potter uses this as the take-off point for a variety of exciting shapes and forms which reflect his personal approach to the medium. The variations of thrown forms shown on this page are examples. A number of thrown shapes can be combined to make one large work, or the symmetry of a thrown bottle can be deliberately distorted by paddling it after it has been removed from the wheel. Forms can be torn and rearranged. Slabs can be added, holes cut, coils circled around. The possibilities are literally endless. The results are rewarding, reflecting as they do the restless search for new, dynamic forms.

Wheel-thrown vase with a thick application of slip texturing. By Reese Bullen. (Right) Wheel-thrown then torn, slab added to build up form. Known as "tear and repair." Porcelain vase by Howard Kottler.

(Above) Combined wheel-thrown base clustered onto a thrown base. Stoneware, slip glazed on top section, 20″ high. By George Kokis.

(Right) Wheel-thrown bottle reshaped by forming convex and concave areas with incise texturing. By Robert Winokur.

Dipping.

Pouring.

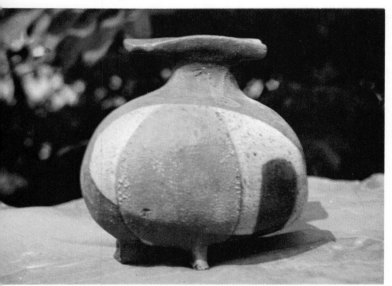

Pot by Sophia and John Fenton.

Bowl by author.

glazing your pots

Following are the four most common methods of applying glaze. Keep in mind that the bottom of a piece is left unglazed, so that it will not stick to the kiln shelf during firing. Either clean off bottom or paint with melted wax before glazing the piece.

Dipping is probably the simplest method, but it requires a large amount of glaze since the bowl or basin used must be full. To glaze a pot one color, hold it at an angle and dip it into the glaze, turning it quickly and holding it so that as much of the pot as possible is covered. Do not let the layer of glaze become too thick. Touch up un-

glazed areas with a brush. When glaze is desired only on the outside of a pot, hold the pot by the base and dip straight up and down. The air trapped inside will prevent the glaze from entering.

Pouring is done when a pot is too large to dip or the amount of glaze available is too little. To coat the inside of a pot, pour glaze in until the pot is one-third filled. Twirl the pot around and pour out the excess. Do this quickly since the correct thickness of freshly applied glaze is that of a playing card. Any more may crack or lump. For the outside, lay the pot on two sticks placed over a basin. Pour glaze evenly over and around the pot.

Spraying.

Brushing.

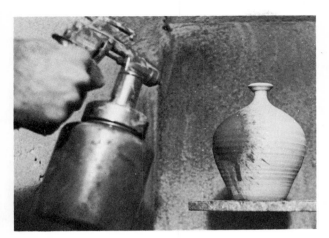

Bottle by Hui Ka Kwong.

Bowl by Ralph Bacerra.

Spraying gives an even coating to the pot and more control over thickness but it often wastes large amounts of glaze. It is recommended chiefly for large pots with deep surface depressions and for applying transparent glazes or colored glaze designs. At times it is hard to tell how thick the glaze is, and the best way to check is by scratching it with a pin. The playing card rule applies also to sprayed glazes.

NOTE: as many glaze materials are toxic, spraying should be done in a booth with an exhaust fan or out of doors.

Brushing is generally used for decorative panels, bands of glaze, etc., but can also be employed for covering an entire pot. Use a wide brush with soft bristles and flow on several coats of glaze for an even application. Apply each coat in a different direction. It is advisable to glaze the inside of a pot first. You can then turn it upside down and work on the outside without disturbing the interior. Oxides or other colorants for decorative designs are best applied with a brush, over the initial glaze if one is used. It helps to have a turntable so that a pot can be rotated while glaze, oxides, and other colorants are being applied.

firing a kiln

Schools, Y.W.C.A.'s, and potteries in your vicinity will often fire your work for a small charge. Or you might consider buying one of the small electric kilns which use regular household current and that are available from ceramic suppliers.

When loading the kiln be sure the glazed pieces are not touching. Always give the kiln a preliminary heating with the door open to allow the chemical water to escape from the clay. Heating time should be at least two hours for raw ware, and more for large or especially heavy pieces.

Let the temperature in the kiln rise gradually and uniformly, for if the pots are heated too quickly, they will explode; let the cooling off time be at least double the firing time. Never open the door of a kiln until the temperature is down to at least 400° F. and never open it completely or attempt to unload a kiln until it has dropped to at least 300° F. Firing to low earthenware temperatures should take eight hours; stoneware needs up to ten.

Before you purchase a small electric kiln, check its voltage to be sure your house wiring circuits are adequate to handle it. Take the same safety precautions in firing a kiln as you would when using any other high voltage appliance.

When buying a kiln, be sure the manufacturer is reliable and is equipped to supply replacement parts.

cones

Cones are a temperature indicator that at a predetermined temperature will melt or bend. Usually these are placed at a slight angle in a piece of clay called a cone pat and put in the kiln in such a position as to be visible through the spyhole when the kiln begins to glow. Use a match or a flashlight to check that the cones are lined up with the spyhole. As soon as the desired kiln temperature is reached the cones will melt and fall over, a signal for the kiln to be turned off.

Pyrometric cones serve as accurate indicators of firing chamber temperature.

CONE TEMPERATURE CHART
(when fired slowly at 68° F. per hour)

Cone Number	Degrees Fahrenheit	Cone Number	Degrees Fahrenheit	Cone Number	Degrees Fahrenheit
022	1085	08	1733	7	2210
021	1103	07	1787	8	2237
020	1157	06	1841	9	2282
019	1166	05	1886	10	2300
018	1238	04	1922	11	2345
017	1328	03	1976	12	2390
016	1355	02	2003	13	2462
015	1418	01	2030	14	2534
014	1463	1	2057	15	2570
013	1517	2	2075	16	2642
012	1544	3	2093	17	2669
011	1607	4	2129	18	2705
010	1634	5	2156	19	2759
09	1706	6	2174	20	2768

PROGRESSIVE FIRING STAGES

Shrinking Chemical water removed	—900° F.
Dehydration Clay changes to pottery	—900°–1300° F.
Oxidation Organic matter burned out	—1300°–1650° F.

KILN PERIODS FOR FIRING TEMPERATURES

Vitrification Red clay Buff clay	C/04–C/4 C/8–C/10
Bisque firing and floor tiles	C/012
Porcelain	C/10–C/20
Lusters and overglazes	C/022–C/010

building your own kiln

A small, inexpensive gas-fired kiln can be constructed for use in your own yard with parts which you can buy new or used. The kiln shown was built by students at The Brooklyn Museum Art School, who were able to find most of the parts second hand and consequently managed to put it in working condition for under $45. Even if you buy everything new, however, you will save more than half of the cost of purchasing a kiln and have the satisfaction of firing your pots in a furnace which you have made. The basic construction is of firebrick, which can possibly be found where houses, apartments, or other buildings are being torn down. The gas line may have to be purchased. The blowers for the air and the rheostats for regulating the amount of air can be obtained at a war surplus store at around $10 each. Ideal blowers come from airplane exhaust systems that operate on regular 1–10 current. The fittings and valves can be bought at a hardware store and then adapted according to the diagram for only a couple of dollars. The burner tips, which are made of clay, can be ordered from Alpine Kiln Co. (see page 95) or any leading kiln supplier.

Open view of kiln.

Complete Kiln Assembly

Cover

Damper

Propane tank

Spy hole

Burner

50-gal. drum

Electric blower

Detail of Blower Unit and Burner

2″ pipe

Electric blower

Gas jet (½″ pipe, 4 holes ⅛″)

Drilled hole ½″ to fit gas jet

Vacuum cleaner (regular 1/10 house current)

Cross Section of Kiln

Cover

Damper

After loading, seal cover with clay

Fire brick

Spy hole

Fire clay and sand mortar

Burner   Blower

Wax-resist decoration

Sgraffito.

Tea set by Paul Masson.

Detail of bowl by Paul Bellardo.

decorating techniques

The methods of surface texture described in earlier sections of this book were for clay still in the plastic state. There are, in addition, ways of decorating clay when it is leather-hard, dry, or even after it has been bisque fired.

Wax-resist decoration can be effectively used when clay is in the dry state or after it has been bisque fired. A design is painted on the clay with a solu-

tion of thinned wax. When glaze is applied, it will run off the wax areas, giving a design in the clay body color surrounded by glaze. The wax need not only be applied to the dry or bisqued clay, but also may be brushed onto a layer of glaze with a second coat of glaze sprayed on top. Any wax can be heated over a hot plate and used. Commercial water-soluble wax emulsions are more convenient but give no better results than any paraffin wax.

Sgraffito is a technique also used on both hard and bisque-fired clay. If wax has been applied, a de-

...ning.

Slip trailing.

...l by John Glick.

Detail of bottle by Anthony Prieto.

...n scratched through the wax with a sgraffito ... gives a sharp linear pattern. More common is ...o scratch a design through the glaze coating of a ...ot to expose either the body or a preliminary ...aze. This is done while the glaze is still slightly ...mp. If too dry or too thick, it will chip and leave ...ragged edge. The object of sgraffito is a sharp, ...ean line.

Staining is best done when the clay is dry. This is a way of treating clay when you want a burnt, natural looking surface. To make a stain, use two tablespoons of any oxide (such as red iron oxide),

the same amount of high or low fire glaze, and half a cup of water. Mix and paint on the area you want stained. Wipe off with a damp sponge. Any impressions in the clay will be darker and the raised surfaces lighter after firing.

Slip trailing is a technique in which slip is trailed over leather-hard clay with a syringe, in much the same way as decorating a cake. The body must not be too dry, however, or the slip will fall off when it dries. A plastic mustard dispenser (shown above) can be as effective as a syringe, and colorants may be added to the slip if desired.

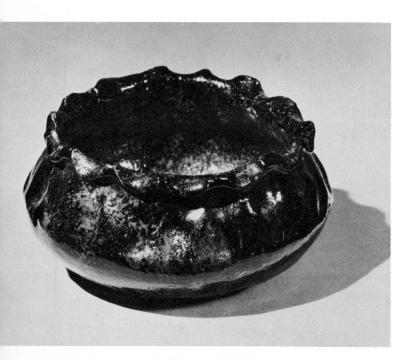

Early Japanese Raku ware bowl. Courtesy of the Brooklyn Museum.

Raku

The Raku method of making pottery was developed by the Japanese and named for the great tea master Sen-no-Rikyu. Although Raku means enjoyment, pleasure, contentment, and ease, the actual forming of Raku is far from the pacific connotations of the word, as it is one of the most dramatic and compelling of the modern potter's techniques. A high fire open clay body is used to make a vessel, which is then bisque fired. (The time-consuming bisque process can be shortened by placing the pot fresh made and wet directly in the red hot kiln to give an instant bisque. Allow no drying to occur, or the pot will explode.) Low-temperature glazes with lead, frit, or borax bases are applied, and the pot is allowed to dry thoroughly. When a kiln has been heated to temperatures somewhere between 1500 and 2000° F., the pot is placed in the red-hot oven with long-handled tongs and left inside until the glaze melts, anywhere from a few minutes to an hour, depending on the temperature of the kiln and the glaze used. The process of the ware is checked through the peep hole in the kiln door, and when the pot looks shiny and wet all over, it is removed from the kiln with tongs. Two things can now be done. The pot can be placed directly in cold water, which will cool it instantly, or it can be plunged into a large container of combustible materials such as sawdust, leaves, or wood chips, and then placed in water to cool.

THE RAKU FIRING PROCESS

With long-handled tongs, remove red hot pot from kiln.

Cover and leave for about 10 minutes.

Smoke-producing materials

REDUCTION GLAZE EFFECT FOR SUBTLE NON-REFLECTING COLORS

Plunge in cold water.

OXIDIZING REACTION FOR BRIGHT, SHINY COLORS

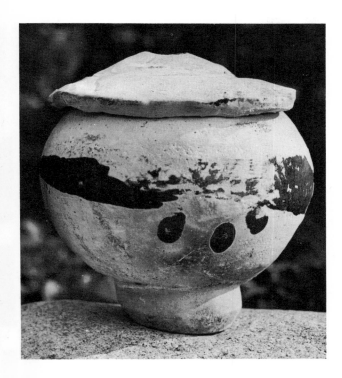

(Above and below) Raku pots, wheel-thrown with engobe decoration. Grey areas developed after firing when pots were exposed to smoke. By Paul Soldner.

(Above) Raku bottle, wheel and slab, 10″ high. The rough texture of the glaze resulted from the Raku firing technique. By the author.

technical notes

Given here are some clay bodies, glazes, and engobes which fire at different temperatures.
Once the base has been weighed, water is added to form a solution—the consistency of light cream.

NOTE: If after firing the unglazed clay body is not as dark in color as you would like, there are two ways to get a darker body: 1) Boil the pot in tea. 2) Use a darkening solution of: 1 teaspoon pyrogallol or pyrogallic acid to 1 pint water. Dunk the pot in the solution or paint it on. It will oxidize in the air in a few hours and give a permanent darker shade. Caution: Avoid direct contact with skin.

CLAY BODIES

Firing-Temperature Range 1922°—2156° F.

C/04–C/5 Cone Range

	Unit of Weight
Jordan Clay	60
Ohio Red Clay	20
Fire Clay	15
Barnard Clay	5

Firing-Temp. Range 2156°–2300°

C/5–C/10

Fire Clay	55
Barnard or Dalton Clay	4
Grog	30
Keystone Ball Clay	8
Bentonite	3

GLAZES

Orange—C/04–1922° F.

	Weights in Grams
White Lead	83.3
Flint	16.0
Potassium Bichromate	6.0
China Clay	8.6
Tin Oxide	5.0

White—C/04–1922° F.

Frit #3304	80
Borax	10
China Clay	5
Colemanite	5
8% Tin Oxide	

For Black add:
3% Red Iron Oxide
2% Cobalt Oxide
2% Manganese Dioxide

Opaque White—C/04–1922° F.

Frit, lead	150.
China Clay	7.5
Zircopax	30.

Glossy White—C/9–2282° F.

Oxford Feldspar	75.
Whiting	12.5
Zinc Oxide	5.

Yellow—C/4–2129° F.

Feldspar, potash	900
Flint	600
China Clay	300
Dolomite	300
Colemanite	600
5% Yellow Stain	
2% Tin Oxide	

Base for Black and Green glazes—C/4-2127°F

Feldspar, potash	120
Kaolin	30
Flint	30
Barium Carbonate	60
Zinc Oxide	30
Colemanite	30

For Black add the following to base:
20% Barnard Clay
5% Copper Carbonate
For Green add to base:
5% Copper Carbonate

Semi-matt—C/9–2282° F

Eureka Spar	15.0
Volcanic Ash	11.5
China Clay	7.0
Silica	7.0
Whiting	12.7
Titanium Oxide	6.2

ENGOBES—ALMOST ANY TEMP. RANGE.

Base, White	Weights in Grams
China Clay	15
Ball Clay	20
Nepheline Syenite	30
Flint	20
Borax	5
Zircopax	5
Talc	5

For Black add:
½% Black Copper Oxide
3% Iron Chromate

For Brown add to base:
3% Red Iron Oxide
10% Rutile

glossary

Absorbtion—Soaking up of water by a clay body.

Ball clay—Highly plastic, fine-grained, sedimentary clay, usually added to less plastic clays.

Bat—A plaster slab or disc on which clay is formed or dried. Made by pouring no less than one inch of plaster into an oiled pie tin.

Biscuit or Bisque—Unglazed clay fired once at a low temperature (cone 010-04).

Calcine—To heat a ceramic material to a moderate temperature to drive off chemical water and carbon dioxide.

Chemical water—Part of the clay that is driven off by heat, causing the clay to shrink in the firing.

China clay—or Kaolin, one of the components of porcelain, a pure clay that fires clear white.

Clay bodies—Prepared clay. The most common classifications are earthenware, stoneware, and porcelain.

Colorants—Various oxides and carbonates which are able to withstand high temperatures and give color to glaze or clay body.

Earthenware—A low firing natural clay body usually red or brown when fired to maturity, non-vitreous and porous with comparatively coarse grain structure and low chipping resistance.

Egyptian paste—A self-glazing body that was used by ancient Egyptian potters.

Engobe—A white or colored thin layer of slip covering a raw or bisque pot, usually to give a harder and smoother surface. It may or may not be glazed over.

Feldspar—Widely found material of several varieties. Orthoclase feldspar, containing potash, is most frequently used in bodies and glazes as an important fluxing agent, and to give a brilliant and waxy appearance to the clay. When decomposed it becomes kaolin.

Flux—Common fluxes are bone ash, frit, feldspar, and lime. They are the lowest melting compound in a glaze.

Frit—A carefully compounded glass which has been fused and fired. Used to render glazes insoluble and make lead non-toxic.

Glaze—Thin coating of special glass, used as a decoration and to seal clay surfaces rendering them waterproof.

Glaze fire—The maturing temperature at which glaze will melt to form a surface coating. Firing ranges vary with the type of glaze.

Grog—Crushed or ground hard-fired clay used to reduce shrinkage or warping and to add texture to the clay.

Incised—Surface designs cut into the clay for decorative purposes.

Kiln—A refractory clay-lined furnace for firing ceramic ware.

Kneading—Wedging or working the clay with fingers to obtain an even texture throughout.

Leather hard—Condition of clay when it is too firm to bend yet soft enough to be carved. Clay in this state can be handled without misshaping it.

Matt glaze—A dull-surfaced glaze, lusterless, and non-reflecting.

Mature—Refers to the development of the desired properties in clays, clay bodies, and glazes.

Overglaze—Decoration of a wear which has already been glazed.

Overglaze colors—Mineral colorants with a lower firing range than the underglazes and not as durable. However the low firing range allows the use of a larger quantity of varied and brilliant colors.

Oxidation—Firing process requiring the presence of oxygen in sufficient quantities to cause combustion of the carbon gases. If not sufficient, some carbon may remain in the ware. A chamber free from smoke and a clear bright flame indicate an oxidized atmosphere.

Peep hole—Small observation hole in kiln wall or door.

Plasticity—The property of clay which allows it to be worked and reshaped without cracking.

Porcelain—Hard and non-porous, the most highly refined of all clay bodies and requiring the highest firing. White, and translucent.

Pottery—Term loosely applied to any ceramic form or to the place where it is made.

Pyrometer—An instrument for recording the exact temperature of the kiln.

Pyrometric cones—Slender pyramids of ceramic material made in a graded series. They do not measure temperature; they measure the amount of heat-work done. At certain temperatures they soften and bend indicating to the potter that the clay and glazes which require a certain time and temperature to mature have done so.

Raku—A method of making pottery using a high-fire, porous clay body. Named for the great tea master Seno-no-Rikyu, it was developed by Japanese potters for the tea ceremony.

Reduction—The cutting down of oxygen to produce a smoky atmosphere in the kiln chamber thus allowing carbon to draw oxygen from the clay body and glazes.

Refractory—Material with a high temperature resistance.

Rib—A tool used in throwing a pot and to smooth surfaces.

Salt glaze—Produced by tossing salt into a hot kiln. The salt vaporizes and combines with the surface of the work.

Sgraffito—From the Italian word meaning "scratched through," done by incising or cutting a design through a colored slip coating to reveal the clay body or a preliminary glaze underneath.

Shrinkage—Contraction of clay during drying or firing.

Slip—Clay in liquid suspension. Functions as a potter's glue or as decoration.

Slip glaze—A raw glaze made from natural clays.

Slip trailing—Decorative process using an eye-dropper, small rubber syringe, or any substitute to trail slip on clay.

Spray booth—An enclosure used when spraying on glazes. Should be well ventilated to prevent inhalation of harmful glaze dust.

Stain—Sometimes a single coloring oxide, but usually a combination of oxides plus alumina, flint, and a fluxing compound. Used in decorating and in coloring glaze.

Stoneware—A hard, vitreous, non-porous, non-translucent body with a wide range of temperature over which it will vitrify. More refined than earthenware and a very useful clay for the potter. Usually buff, tan, or grey when fired.

Throwing—Forming pottery on the wheel.

Translucency—Ability of a clay body to transmit scattered light.

Vitreous—Impurities in the clay which melt upon heating to form glass and act as a bond.

Ware—Pottery in either raw, bisque, or glazed state.

Warping—Distortion in a pot caused by non-uniform drying or uneven ware thickness, or from being fired in a kiln which does not heat evenly.

Wax resist—A method of decoration using warm wax or a wax emulsion applied to either raw or bisque pots or between two layers of glaze. Wax applied to the pot will resist the glaze and will lift off after firing.

Weathering—Rendering the clay more plastic by exposing it to all types of weather.

Wedging—The process of vigorously forcing any air bubbles from the clay in order to obtain a uniform consistency.

schools

Following is a partial listing of professional schools, universities, and workshops that offer courses in ceramics. Since some courses are seasonal it's best to check with the individual school. Also investigate your local high school or craft center.

Troy State University
Art Dept.
Troy, **Alabama** 36081

Art Center School
300 No. Main Avenue
Tucson, **Arizona** 85705

University of California
Dept. of Design
234 Wurster Hall
Berkeley, **California** 94720

Pond Farm Pottery
Box 322
Guerneville, **California** 95446

University of Southern California
Idyllwild School of Music and the Arts
Idyllwild, **California** 92349

Barnsdall Art & Craft Center
4800 Hollywood Blvd.
Los Angeles, **California** 90027

The Mendocino Art Center
540 Little Lake Street
P.O. Box 36
Mendocino, **California** 95460

California College of Arts & Crafts
5212 Broadway
Oakland, **California** 94618

Richmond Art Center
Civic Center Plaza
Richmond, **California** 94804

Southern Colorado State College
400 W. Orman Avenue
Pueblo, **Colorado** 81005

Brookfield Craft Center, Inc.
Brookfield, **Connecticut** 06804

Wesleyan Potters, Inc.
350 So. Main Street
Middletown, **Connecticut** 06457

American University of Art
Dept. of Art
Massachusetts & Nebraska Aves. NW
Washington, **D.C.** 20016

Pottery Workshop at Rising Fawn
The Pottery Shop
Route 2
Rising Fawn, **Georgia** 30738

School of the Art Institute of Chicago
Michigan & Adams
Chicago, **Illinois** 60603

Gary Artists' League
400 So. Lake Street
Gary, **Indiana** 46403

Herron School of Art
of Indiana University
1701 No. Pennsylvania Street
Indianapolis, **Indiana** 46202

Friends of Art
1737 West 12th Street
Davenport, **Iowa** 52804

Des Moines Art Center
Greenwood Park
Des Moines, **Iowa** 50312

Wichita Art Association, Inc.
9112 East Central
Wichita, **Kansas** 67206

Berea College
Art Dept.
Berea, **Kentucky** 40403

Haystack Mountain School of Crafts
Deer Isle, **Maine** 04627

Workshops in Creative Crafts
Boston YWCA
140 Clarendon Street
Boston, **Massachusetts** 02116

De Cordova Museum School of Art
Sandy Pond Road
Lincoln, **Massachusetts** 01773

Craft Center
25 Sagamore Road
Worcester, **Massachusetts** 01650

Bloomfield Art Association
1516 So. Cranbrook Road
Birmingham, **Michigan** 48009

Cranbrook Academy of Art
500 Lone Pine Road
Box 806
Bloomfield Hills, **Michigan** 48013

Rochester Art Center
320 E. Center Street
Rochester, **Minnesota** 55901

University of Missouri
Dept. of Art
A 126 Fine Arts
Columbia, **Missouri** 65201

Kansas City Art Institute
4415 Warwick Blvd.
Kansas City, **Missouri** 64111

Essayons Studio, Inc.
8725 Big Bend Blvd.
St. Louis, **Missouri** 63119

Manchester Institute of
Arts & Sciences
148 Concord Street
Manchester, **New Hampshire** 03104

Weiss Studio & Workshop
161 Culberson Road
Basking Ridge, **New Jersey** 07920

Peters Valley Crafts School
Peters Valley Village
Layton, **New Jersey** 07851

Newark Museum Arts Workshop
43–49 Washington Street
Newark, **New Jersey** 07101

State University of New York
College of Ceramics
at Alfred University
Alfred, **New York** 14802

Brooklyn Museum Art School
200 Eastern Parkway
Brooklyn, **New York** 11238

Great Neck Public School
Adult Education
10 Arrandale Avenue
Great Neck, **New York** 11024

Crafts Student League
West Side Branch YWCA
840 8th Avenue
New York, **New York** 10019

Penland School of Crafts
Penland, **North Carolina** 28765

Temple University
Tyler School of Art
Beech & Penrose Avenues
Philadelphia, **Pennsylvania** 19126

Arrowmont School of Arts & Crafts
P.O. Box 567
Gatlinburg, **Tennessee** 37738

Visual Gravity at Potomac Stoneware
417 No. Union Street
Alexandria, **Virginia** 22314

Pottery Northwest, Inc.
Seattle Center
305 Harrison Street
Seattle, **Washington** 98109

University of Puget Sound
1500 No. Lawrence Street
Tacoma, **Washington** 98447

Canada:

Banff School of Fine Arts
Banff, Alberta, **Canada**

Elliot Lake Centre
for Continuing Education
Elliot Lake, Ontario, **Canada**

bibliography

BOOKS:

EPPENS, J. H. *Pottery*. Universe Books, New York, New York, 1964.
LEACH, Bernard. *A Potter's Book*. Transatlantic Arts, Inc., Levittown, New York, 1967.
MARLOW, Reginald, A.R.C.A. *Pottery Making and Decorating*. Studio Publications, New York, New York, 1957.
NELSON, Glenn C. *Ceramic Reference Manual*. Burgess Publishing Co., Minneapolis, Minnesota, 1958.
NELSON, Glenn C. *Ceramics, A Potter's Handbook*. Holt, Rinehart & Winston, Inc., New York, New York, 1971, 3rd edition.
NOBLE, Joseph V. *The Techniques of Painted Attic Pottery*. Watson-Guptill Publications, Inc., New York, New York, 1965.
NORTON, F. H. *Ceramics, An Illustrated Primer*. Hanover House, New York, New York, 1960.
RHODES, Daniel. *Clay and Glazes for the Potter*. Chilton Book Co., Philadelphia, Pennsylvania, 1957.
SANDERS, Herbert H. *The World of Japanese Ceramics*. Kodansha Int'l., Palo Alto, California, 1967.
WILDENHAIN, Marguerite. *Pottery: Form and Expression*. Reinhold Publishing Corp., New York, New York, 1962.

MAGAZINES:

Craft Horizons A bimonthly publication of the American Craftsmen's Council, 16 East 52nd Street, New York, New York, 10022

Ceramics Monthly P.O. Box 4548, Columbus, Ohio, 43212

FILM SERVICES:

Research and Education Dept., American Crafts Council, 29 West 53rd Street, New York, New York 10019

suppliers

CLAYS, KILNS, AND EQUIPMENT

The following is a list of some of the major ceramic suppliers to whom you can write for catalogues. For small amounts of materials try local building and supply dealers, and craft shops.

General:

The Craftool Co., Inc.
1421 West 240th St.
Harbor City, **California** 90710

Garden City Clay Co.
Redwood City, **California** 94064

Western Ceramic Supply Co.
1601 Howard Street
San Francisco, **California** 94103

Denver Fire Clay Co.
3033 Blake Street
Denver, **Colorado** 80205

Western Stoneware Co.
Monmouth, **Illinois** 61462

American Art Clay Co.
4717 West 16th Street
Indianapolis, **Indiana** 46222

Newton Pottery Supply Co.
Newton, **Massachusetts** 01432

Jack D. Wolfe Co., Inc.
724–734 Meeker Avenue
Brooklyn, **New York** 11222

Stewart Clay Co., Inc.
133 Mulberry Street
New York, **New York** 10013

U.S. Stoneware Co.
Akron, **Ohio** 44309

George Fetzer Ceramic Supply Co.
1205 17th Avenue
Columbus, **Ohio** 43211

Kentucky Tennessee Clay Co.
Mayfield, **Ohio** 42066

Cedar Heights Clay Co.
50 Portsmouth Road
Oak Hill, **Ohio** 45656

Standard Ceramics Supply Co.
P.O. Box 4435
Pittsburgh, **Pennsylvania** 15205

Pottery Supply House
491 Wildwood Road
P.O. Box 192
Oakville, Ontario, **Canada**

Mercedes Ceramics Supply
8 Wallace Street
Woodbridge, Ontario, **Canada**

Kilns:

A. D. Alpine, Inc.
353 Coral Circle
El Segundo, **California** 90245

Harrop Ceramic Service Co.
35 E. Gay Street
Columbus, **Ohio** 43215

W. H. Fairchild
712 Centre Street
Freeland, **Pennsylvania** 18224